WINTERDANCE

❄ ❄ ❄

The Fine Madness
of Running the Iditarod

WINTERDANCE

✳ ✳ ✳

The Fine Madness
of Running the Iditarod

GARY PAULSEN

A Harvest Book • Harcourt, Inc.

San Diego   New York   London

Library of Congress Cataloging-in-Publication Data
Paulsen, Gary.
Winterdance: the fine madness of running the Iditarod/Gary
Paulsen.—1st ed.
p.   cm.
ISBN 0-15-600145-4
1. Paulsen, Gary.   2. Iditarod Trail Sled Dog Race, Alaska.
3. Mushers—Alaska—Autobiography.   I. Title.   II. Title:
Winterdance.
SF440.15.P38   1994
798.8'092—dc20   93-42096
[B]

Designed by Kaelin Chappell

Printed in the United States of America
First Harvest edition 1995

S T

To the Iditarod volunteers,
who make the race happen.

Contents

© A·Karl/J·Kemp, 19

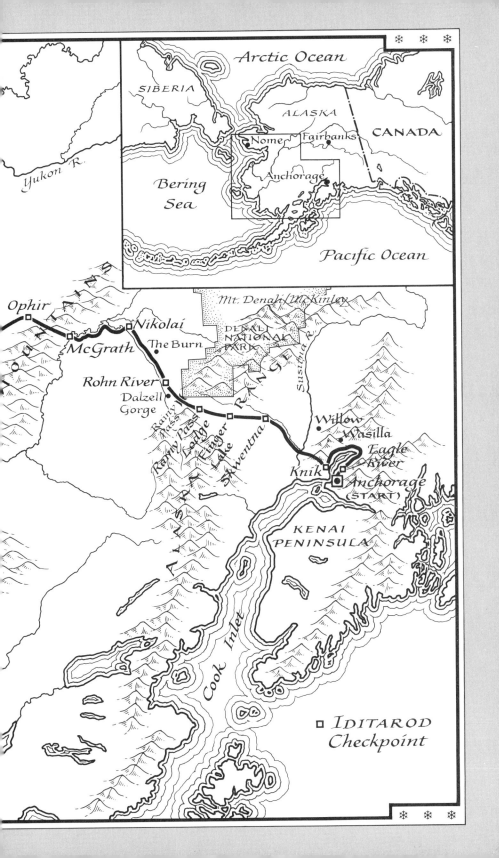

Arctic Ocean

SIBERIA

ALASKA

CANADA

Nome   Fairbanks

Anchorage

Bering Sea

Yukon R.

Pacific Ocean

Mt. Denali/McKinley

Ophir

Nikolai

McGrath   The Burn

DENALI NATIONAL PARK

Rohn River

Dalzell Gorge

Rainy Pass

Rainy Pass Lodge

Finger Lake

Skwentna

Susitna R.

Willow

Wasilla

Eagle River

Knik

Anchorage
(START)

KENAI PENINSULA

Cook Inlet

☐ IDITAROD
    Checkpoint

Prelude

The storm broke with a sudden viciousness that startled, frightened me.

I had left camp with eight dogs and a lightly loaded sled just after midnight. They were my "problem" dogs. In all teams there are good dogs, some not-so-good dogs, and then there are "problem" dogs: dogs that might be a bit young, or like to fight too much, or spend too much time looking back to see what the sled driver is doing. They require extra effort, the problem dogs—more time to understand, time to know, time to learn how they think and act and work.

So, once every four days or so I would harness the problem dogs and head up a mountain and try to learn from them and about them. We were in Alaska to train three months before my second Iditarod race, and I was learning as much as the dogs.

The difficulty came because of a headache. Simple things, small things change lives. My winter cap had fallen in the fire and burned. I bought a new one but it had more bulk, a thicker weave. When I left camp I put my battery pack on my waist and the band for the headlamp around my head and over the cap so the light was centered on my forehead. It was too tight because the hat was more bulky. The band was adjusted as far out as it would go, and to fix it I would have to sew on a piece of cloth to extend it.

But the dogs were already harnessed and hooked in the gangline and screaming to run in the high-pitched keening shrillness that demanded hurrying, so without changing the headband I stood to the sled and un-hooked from the birch tree that held it.

They ran well at first, excited by the run. I left camp and headed north and east, up into the moun-tains that marked the end of the Alaska Range. As the trail steepened and the snow grew more powdery with altitude, the dogs slowed and settled in for the long haul over the pass.

An hour passed, whuffling along in the dogs' breath, the runners sighing. Everything—everything with the dogs, with the country, with my life, with each breath, everything was beautiful. But I didn't, couldn't see it.

I was in agony. My head was throbbing from the tight band on the headlamp and I wasn't seeing beauty, dogs, sled, country—any of it. The Chinese have a proverb that says a man with a toothache cannot be in love and that concept was very much driving me.

My temples ached and the pain worked around my head, warping my thinking to keep me not only from enjoying the run but from watching warning signs, paying attention to the dogs, and when I finally started to see things it was too late by far.

They tried—the dogs, the trees, the wind. When I stopped to check dog feet and work in ointment a big, white, slab-sided dog named Crackers started fidgeting, smelling the breeze that was now and then gusting into wind. I didn't understand it, didn't see it for the warning it was.

Flakes of snow—not large and fluffy but small and mean, driven—started to appear. They were a sign of weather coming, as was Crackers's restlessness (he hated storms and liked to be well holed up before they hit), but I ignored the snow as well, finished working on their feet, and called the dogs up as soon as I'd finished.

I had in mind finishing the run. Making some kind of loop—eighty or ninety miles—and getting done with it and back into camp and comfort where I could sew a new band for the headlamp (or the goddamn headlamp, as I was beginning to think of it) and I had, in my misdirected focusing on my own small problem, completely forgotten some of the basic tenets of running dogs. The most important: your home is where you are with the team, the sled. You cannot outrun weather. Or, as I had heard one musher say: you've got to dance even when the music sucks.

The music was souring. The wind was increasing exponentially. It had lacked purpose for a time, wallowed this way and that, but now it had direction and some force. And the sleet had increased as well; not completely obscuring vision yet—I could still see the team pretty well in the yellow/white spot of the headlamp—but definitely more than it had been. Another warning.

And still I ignored it and worse, far worse, by ignoring it I did things to compound the error.

I went through a tight stand of dense spruce. They were set thickly and blocked the wind completely, and some of them were dead and would make wonderful firewood. I could have stopped here and tipped the sled and pulled a tarp over the top to make a nearly perfect shelter; could have made a fire at the mouth with wood enough to last a week all within easy reach; could have laid out a foam pad, pulled a few dogs inside with me, and ridden out the storm in complete comfort. I had four cans of beef stew and forty-five pounds of meat for the dogs, and we could have lived well even with storm rationing.

Could have.

Instead my head was getting pinched and I passed through the trees without noticing them, or at least without thinking of what they could mean to me and to the dogs. Shelter, warmth, hope . . .

Life.

At the end of the stand of spruce the trail left timberline and headed into the snowfields of the high country. In truth there wasn't much of a trail—more just a line or more often no mark at all in the snow and I was depending on the lead dog, a tiny female named Duberry, to find the way. She was good at it, sometimes going by feel as she trotted, quick and alert, her little black and white form tugging out front like a beacon.

Just as the trail left the trees it moved into a shallow depression and went along the side of the mountain for two miles or so, angled so that I had to stand on one runner and pull the sled over at an angle to keep it from sliding down the mountain.

This put my parka back to the wind and that, coupled with being in the depression and having the headache, made me not notice further warnings. The wind was much stronger now, straight in line and with no eddies, getting force from somewhere, going to somewhere, reaching the point where small things would start to become very, very important. Little ignorances, small sillinesses, a loose bolt, a dropped mitten could cripple, could kill.

At the end of the depression the trail moved out into partial open, still slight around the side of the mountain, but where there could be no shelter and anybody except a complete idiot would know the seriousness of the wind, the storm.

But I hunkered with my back to it all, my head thunking away, staring down at the runner next to me, while I stood on the other sideways and wished to hell I had taken time to make the headband longer for another mile, then another, then another . . .

Seven, eight miles out into the snowfields above timberline, away from shelter, away from heat and comfort, away from rest.

And into madness.

I had turned three-quarters away from the wind, not just back to it but looking to the rear down the trail, half bemused that our tracks were blowing and filling before the sled had gone eight feet, which was about as far as I could see in the blowing snow and wind.

Here some survival code kicked in, some nudge in my thoughts that if the tracks were filling that fast the wind must be getting worse . . .

Right then Duberry took the team out around the side of the mountain and it was like passing around the end of a wall.

Duberry simply vanished.

I had swung around and looked forward as we came out into the true open just in time to see a churning cloud of white hit her from the side like a bulldozer. For an instant I thought she was merely obscured by snow and squinted, trying to see through the roiling mass and the suddenly shrieking wind, but it was impossible.

She was gone.

Blown away to the side, and in a heartbeat the sled and the rest of the team were carried by momentum into the roar and were gone as well.

I grabbed, snatched with my hand as the wind hit but it was too sudden, too wild, and I was torn from the sled, taken by the wind, tumbling end over end down the mountain.

Velocities, technical terms are meaningless. I knew a man who tried to make a winter ascent of Mt. Denali/McKinley who was blown off the mountain, lost and dead and gone and the body never found and some estimated that the wind had to be one fifty, two hundred miles an hour to carry a human body sideways off a mountain.

I do not know how fast the wind was blowing. I have never—including two typhoons in the Philippines—been in anything remotely like the force that took me now; I had, literally, no control over my life.

It simply blew me sideways from the sled. I tried to hook my elbow in the handlebar but I missed, and I had a glimpse of the sled swinging like a weather vane, hanging downwind from the team, and then nothing.

I tried to stand but the wind kept knocking me down, tumbling me end over end down the mountain. I would try to grab hold but there was nothing to catch and I just kept rolling and bouncing. I'm not sure how long it lasted. I was completely disoriented, had only the vaguest idea of up and down and could see nothing, hear nothing but the scream of the wind.

It could have blown me anywhere it wanted, blown me to hell, blown me off the world and I wouldn't have known it.

Instead it fetched me up against a rocky outcropping covered with ice. I hit with a thump that knocked the air out of my lungs, burying my head in a mound of snow. I hung there for seconds, perhaps half a minute, held by the pressure of the wind pushing me against the ice and rock and thinking started to come back in jerks.

Dogs. The dogs. Where were the dogs? Were they all right?

"Duberry!"

I tried to call, yell her name but the wind tore it away. I was still on my side, half raised, and I used my mittened hands like claws to hold to the rocks while I edged around to the side, searching for a place that was out of the blast.

Inches at a time. Once my foot seemed to hang out over space and the wind lifted my leg, floated it up and I jerked it back down, slithered a bit and came around beneath a slight overhang and for the first time caught my breath and felt as if I might be able to hold the position.

It was, I thought, the way people died—what I was doing. Little things, small things, kill. I was partially out of the wind but I had no gear apart from my clothing, no food, no fuel, no . . . anything.

It happened just this way. Caught in wind, cold, blowing snow, confused enough to forget life, and death came. Winds in high country sometimes lasted days, weeks, and I was locked in, caught in back of the small rock face, lost.

There were moments of self-pity and anger at how stupid I had become. To compound my problem my batteries were going down fast and my headlamp was very dim. I had fresh batteries in a bag on the sled but . . .

Then instinct took over and I tried to make the best of what I had. In the slight yellow glow and eddying snow, dumped by the wind as it came over the rock, I saw that the opening went back in slightly—a foot and a half—beneath the overhang. The hole was filled with hard-packed snow and I started digging, making almost no impression in the frozen snow, when I felt a presence.

This had happened before, when hallucinating, and it was all in my mind. In truth I was tired and not thinking straight and I looked around once and then decided it was just that, my dreams catching up with me again, and ignored it.

But the feeling persisted. Something was there, was close. Something or someone. And I couldn't ignore it. I stopped digging and turned, tried to see in the wall of snow and wind but couldn't and yet felt if I just stretched, just moved away from the shelter a little bit, a tiny distance . . .

Insane. To leave the shelter. If anything the wind was worse and if I moved into the open it would take me again, sweep me away.

Yet I couldn't resist the pull. It was there, something, something close—I knew it absolutely and I scrabbled around on my stomach, pulled away from the shelter a few inches, a foot, hung on the edge of the wind with my left hand and the toe of my left foot dug into holes in the snow to hold me, teetered there and was about to give up when I saw it.

A shape. A triangular shape in the snow, sitting there, wobbling and weaving in the wind.

The sled.

Sitting upright, taking the full force of the storm and not moving, the sled was right in front of me, not four feet away. It simply couldn't be there, should have been blown for miles, but it sat there, as if waiting for me to ride.

For a second I couldn't believe it—laws of physics were being challenged. A goddamn tank wouldn't have been able to sit there in that wind.

Yet it was there and I crawled on my stomach until I could touch the end of the runner to convince myself it was real, and when I was close I saw what had happened.

Luck. All luck. As the sled tumbled, the snow-hook—the sharp anchor tied into the gangline to hold the dogs when the sled is stopped—had bounced out of the leather carrying pouch and dragged along the snow. It was the kind of hook that is self-burying, like an anchor on a boat, biting deeper the harder it is pulled, but it had not set in the snow. Instead it had skittered along in some way until it came to the rocks and then caught in a small crack that captured both sides of the hook.

The team was there as well. I couldn't see them but they were still tied to the sled, strung down the mountain with the wind pulling at them, and I had been given life where there was almost no hope.

But to live, to make it work, I would have to leave the shelter and work down the team and bring them back up to the rock and all the while I would be dependent on the hook holding. If it popped loose it would all start over, the wind would own us, and we would be gone once more and there couldn't be the kind of luck again that would catch the hook just where it needed to catch. I lay looking at the rope and the hook, trying not to think of the risk, the gamble, but thinking of the other things that were important and I knew that it wasn't me, it wasn't just me anymore.

It was us.

I could take the pad and sleeping bag and food out of the sled and drag them back into the hole and make a shelter and live through it. I would be all right. I would even perhaps be comfortable. I.

But the dogs were out in it. Out in the wind. And with their backs to it the wind would blow the hairs open, drive snow and sleet down into the hair and closer to their bodies, and their body temperatures would go down. I had been told by other dog drivers. If their body temperatures went down they could start building fluid on their lungs, get pneumonia—it could kill them. They might get me home but they might die even then.

And there came a moment—lying on my stomach looking at the hook that I was holding in place with my hands in the faint glow from my dying headlamp— came a moment when I knew I couldn't allow that. In some way we had gone past where that could be allowed, gone past where I could have lived with myself, gone into an area where it had become we, instead of I.

For another minute my body rebelled. Everything in me fought against getting up, depending on that hook caught in the crack, and working my way down the team to pull them back in with me. It was not a sensible act.

But it happened. My legs moved, pushed me half up—still almost against my will. I hammered at the hook with both hands, trying to set the point deeper in the crack, grabbed the sled, and moved out into the wind.

It had, if anything, increased in ferocity. It worked inside my parka hood, seemed to pluck at my eyelids and drive snow under them and it tore me loose once more, drove me down along the gangline, clutching at the main rope as I moved through the dogs, who were in an unholy mess. They had tumbled in the wind themselves, blown ahead of the wind, and had tangled and retangled until some of them were upside down with all four feet caught in their tugs.

I worked dog to dog, going by feel. My light was gone now, not even a glow, but I had unharnessed and harnessed enough to know how the ropes and tugs and necklines should feel to the touch. As I untangled each dog it stood, its back to the wind, and waited and at last I came to Duberry, the only one not tangled. She was curled in a small ball in the snow and was reluctant to get up but I pulled at her collar and started up the slope, dragging her with me, clawing, heaving until at last I was back in the small shelter of the overhang with her.

Duberry's tug was hooked back into the gangline and she had been pulling the other dogs back and around and up with her. I put her to the side and kept pulling, putting each dog down next to her as they came to me until we were all there, crammed in the small space.

They were demoralized by the wind and two started to fight, which triggered more fighting, and I cursed and screamed and cuffed until they were relatively quiet once again.

Then I grabbed the main gangline and pulled the nose of the sled back and around and to me—all still in the dark—and tipped it on its side so the body of the sled would block some of the wind coming around the edge of the rock.

We now had the start of a shelter, the rock making the biggest wall, the sled stopping the eddies on the upwind corner, and the dogs forming the rest on the downwind side.

I unzipped the sled bag and took out my sleeping bag and foam pads, pulling them under me, then tucked myself into the sleeping bag and pulled dogs around and in and on top of me until I was covered with a living mass of fur.

Of course they would not all fit but I jammed the ones I could in on top of me and huddled in. They were at least out of the wind and comfortable on the sleeping bag and foam pad and we settled in to ride out the storm.

All of this took less than half an hour, just reacting to weather and wind, and I had not actually tried to think things through. In the shelter with the dogs on top of me I started to think and I realized that if the storm lasted for a long time nobody would come looking for me for two or three days, if then, and that if there was a solution to my problem—if, indeed, I *had* a problem—it would have to come from me. From the dogs and me.

I was alone.

Always in my life there had been something else, someone else. There had been bad times, rough times, but there had somehow always been other people. But not now.

It was, at the very first, frightening and then a secondary feeling came, a kind of liberation that I did not understand. It made no sense. I was in a snow shelter in the Alaska Range in the middle of the worst storm I had ever seen with no possible chance of external help and I felt liberated.

The dogs rested for a time but they were not tired and being jammed one on another when it was not time to rest or stop made them uneasy. They have definite likes and dislikes and will often hate each other—especially females—for no apparent good reason. Jamming them in one on another, tangling them, is sometimes dangerous when they aren't tired. They started to fidget and fight and within moments my clothes were torn and I was bleeding where I had been bitten. I bellowed at them and swore and they settled again—with uneasy growls at each other—and I returned to my thoughts.

I decided the reason I felt liberated was that there is a kind of freedom in being alone. It was true I could die, the dogs could die—we had food for three days and maybe I could run another four or five with no food, but if the storm dropped several feet of snow and it was soft I would have to move in front of the dogs on snowshoes to make a trail and it would be too much work for too long. Eighty to a hundred miles, at best a mile an hour, maybe half a mile an hour breaking trail . . .

Math while covered with dogs in a snow shelter waiting out a storm: If you broke trail with snowshoes at half a mile an hour and it was eighty miles to camp—where there was food for the dogs—it would take 160 hours.

Cook of Antartica, who was a fool and didn't believe in dogs, died eleven miles from his food.

The dogs moved and scrabbled again and I growled at them. I was starting to growl more and more at them and talk less. Speaking in grunts.

So, if it took 160 hours in normal weather, what would it take if you were truly alone and free and another storm came up while you were trying to get back? What would it take if two trains left Chicago and there were storms and their lead dogs developed bad feet and they simply could not move and there was no food?

It was still too soon in my dog career for me to begin to go mad while running them. That would come later. But the initial phases of the madness, the focus and primitive sharpness, the instincts were there, and when time became long beneath the dogs, hour after hour and the storm had not stopped, my thinking began to roll by itself, tumbling and falling until the heat from the dogs and my bag caught up with the strain and tiredness and I slept.

I'm not sure how long I slept. Initially it was light and the dogs kept hassling, but soon I went into deep REM sleep and was aware of nothing until I felt pain in my eyes.

It was sharp, defined—like needles—and I awakened to a thin shaft of flashbulb-bright white light drilling directly into my eyes through a hole between Duberry, who was on my head, and a dog named Walter, who was across my chest and lower chin.

I moved my head and shoulders and the dogs felt me and yawned and stretched on top of me and then stood and shook, and I saw the world through a shower of snow that had drifted and heaped on top of the dogs.

It had not snowed much but had blown deep drifts here and there and I sat up and saw that the outcropping where we sheltered was between two drifts ten or so feet high.

I unzipped the bag and stood and saw for the first time in daylight where I was.

It was dazzling. Before, above, and out to the northwest lay the whole Alaska Range. It's possible to live a month below McKinley and the range and never see them through the clouds, but there wasn't a cloud in the sky and the peaks looked like they were right on top of me.

It was still, not a breath of wind, and deeply, intensely cold. Forty-five, perhaps fifty below. I shook snow out of the bag and zipped it and rolled it, then I flipped the sled up and knocked snow off the cloth sled bag. I had a stove cooker inside and decided since the weather was clear and looked to stay clear for a while I would take time to cook food and feed the dogs.

I pulled out the food bag and the stove and soon had the five-gallon aluminum cooker melting snow and heating meat chunks for the dogs. I fed them and lined them out on the snow and untangled them and re-hooked those that had unhooked and loaded the sled and then saw just exactly how close I had been.

Two things, both possibly fatal:

The hook, which I had depended on when I made my way down the dogs to drag them back into shelter—the hook had popped and hung by only one tiny corner of rock caught on the very tip of the left hook prong.

It wobbled there, barely caught, and as I reached down for it the movement of my hand brushing it loosened it the rest of the way and the hook fell away. It had been that close when I went to get the dogs—that fragile a thread had held me.

And when I stood to the sled and called the team up, started working back the way we had come, squinting because I hadn't brought sunglasses, I saw what would have happened had the hook come loose.

Below us, where the wind would have driven us, lay a huge canyon. The wind had been blowing us toward the canyon wall, which dropped several hundred feet nearly vertically to a frozen river.

I would not, could not have survived the fall without serious damage and any damage would have been fatal. Lying in the bottom of the canyon, broken, the dogs gone as well—none of us would have made it.

The hook had caught, blown the team down until they hung on the gangline still attached to the hook— the hook had caught with Duberry not fifty feet from the edge of the canyon wall. Taking into account the drift that hung out over the edge now, she was almost on top when the hook stopped her.

All luck.

Everything had been done wrong. Not fixing the headband on the lamp, not replacing batteries, not stopping where I should have stopped, moving into unknown territory in bad weather—all stupid mistakes, mistakes that had injured and killed people, and luck had kicked in, saved us.

The snow wasn't inordinately deep except in the drifts and we could move around those. I let them run until they settled and immersed myself in the run and the beauty of the mountains. We were high enough to see almost all of the country back down to Willow and Anchorage, spread out like an impossibly beautiful map below us. The dogs were running well, shoulders driving, all the tugs tight and the absence of wind made the night before seem like a bad dream.

It did not hit me until later. Much later. We finished the run and the dogs were tied back in camp sleeping on straw and I was sitting with a friend sipping tea, looking at the fire cooking a fifty-five-gallon barrel full of dog meat and mush. The heat from the fire made my face seem to burn and I raised the cup of tea and my hands were shaking.

"Cold?" my friend asked.

I put the cup down but kept staring into the fire. "No. Scared."

"Scared of what?"

I had told him some of what happened but not how close it had been, not how the hook looked hanging by one prong, not how the canyon yawned away forever down and down and how the wind blew and how really, really goddamn close it had been. All of it rushed in now and I looked at the tea, thinking I would take a drink in a minute, when the shaking had subsided a bit.

"Just scared—you know. Life. All of it."

And because he had been in the military and seen and done those things and had lived long enough to know, he did not ask more. He nodded, and we sat staring into the fire and I thought that any sane man who was in his forties and had a good career going would quit now, would leave the dogs, end it now and go back to the world and sanity and I knew what scared me wasn't the canyon and wasn't the hook hanging by one prong but the knowledge, the absolute fundamental knowledge that I could not stop, would not stop, would never be able to stop running dogs of my own free will.

THE DOGS

Beginnings

I had been running dogs for almost a year, through the winter.

Random patterns — the wonderful variance of events that makes life so unpredictable — had been pushing me for two years to bring me to this point. Starting in Colorado, breaking my family and me financially, driving us north to find a cheap place to live, settling us in a shack in the northern woods of Minnesota, breaking us still further financially so that we had no transportation until somebody gave me four dogs and a broken sled and I started to hunt and trap with them. So we lived and I began to run dogs for transportation and work and, finally, for joy.

I did not actually ever decide that I would go to Alaska and run the Iditarod.

We were content to live as we had come to live, gardening, hunting some, trapping some, farming some—just living and trying to have a measure of quality in each part of our lives.

We had carried this concept to the point that at one time I thought that if I could just grow a perfect tomato (it never happened and still hasn't though I continue to try) I would be as happy as I would be about anything.

But I began to notice the dogs. As I spent more time with them, trapping, bringing in firewood—we burned sixteen cords of oak a year, for cooking and heat, all brought in by dogs—living, watching them, I began to have a feeling for the true sanctity of life, began to understand that life is all the cosmos gives and that to remove it, from anything, is incorrect.

This did not happen instantly but over the winter, using dogs to live, watching them think, knowing them, and talking to an old man who had been a cowboy in Montana.

He talked about cows. At the time we ate beef, raised and slaughtered and cooked our own, and I did not think of cattle as having life in some way. They plodded, they lived, they occupied space, but in some way I thought of them as Al Capp's little schmoos— nonthinking, nonbeing sources of protein; enormous protozoa. Not having the same life as humans. But the old cowboy sat in our house by the stove and drank coffee and told us of how range cows got what he called "grass smart." The cows and their calves would range far from water while they were eating. Sometimes three or four miles from water. The calves didn't need water because they had the milk from the cows, but every other day or so the cows would have to go to water. The problem was the calves couldn't make the trip to water and back each time, and they couldn't be left alone because the coyotes would be at them without an adult to protect them, and it would seem to be an impossible situation.

The cows solved it by selecting one of their own to stay with the calves and babysit while the others went to water. Even this was not perhaps so astonishing. But then he told us that they kept a roster and the same cow didn't stay each time but a different one, and they always knew which cow was due to stay, and right about then Ruth had her last taste of meat and I stopped trapping and killing and hunting.

But the beauty of the woods, the incredible joy of it is too alluring to be ignored, and I could not stand to be away from it—indeed, still can't—and so I ran dogs simply to run dogs; to be in and part of the forest, the woods.

Some thought I still trapped and I let them think so—caught in a kind of guilt that just to be running dogs for the sake of running them was to fritter away time—but I was just going to go, and a change came with running them.

It was in some strange manner abrupt but gradual at the same time and it had to do with beauty.

I would see a thing of beauty when running them, or many things, the pictures like frozen jewelry, and there would not be so much beauty when not running them. So I ran them because I wanted to see the beauty again, find the wonderful places they could take me.

Like the tandem lakes . . .

Three small lakes, set perfectly in an immense forest of Norway pines, and beaver houses on the lakes that were never trapped, never touched because it was too far in to walk, not possible to drive in, and snowmachines could not get through the terrain—swamp and thick brush. But the dogs could weave through, and I spent many days on those lakes, gliding silently along shore on the work sledge with the chickadees and snowbirds flitting around me. The lakes were so perfect, so clean, so pristine that they seemed almost artificial; like the scenes in those glass tip-over globes where the snow falls softly in the fluid.

We rounded a bend in the lakes one January afternoon, crisp cold, and I saw a figure on the ice ahead of us. It was a beaver, large enough to be what is termed "a blanket" in trapping circles—perhaps sixty or seventy pounds. What on earth he was doing above the ice was a mystery. Beavers almost always spend the whole winter beneath the ice, living in their houses with underwater entrances, storing food under the ice, and coming up only to take limbs (and corn, if they live near a cornfield) back into their houses to eat quietly. But here he was, walking unconcernedly across the lake.

The dogs saw him as well and headed directly for him and I couldn't stop them. The work sledge I used had a crude steel claw for a brake, which wouldn't bite on the ice, and I jumped on the damn thing with both feet but it just bounced on the lake ice. Ice has many consistencies depending on how it was frozen and how cold it is, but at twenty or thirty below—as it was now—it is as hard and brittle as marble and the brakes, the snowhook, dragging my feet were all worthless. I even took my hunting knife out of the sledge and tried stabbing the point in the ice, clawing at it, trying to stop.

I knew some about beaver. They have the press of being soft, friendly animals that spend all their time making ponds and houses and chewing down trees. That is in some measure true. But they are also enormously strong and those front teeth—they can and often do chew oak trees down although they do not eat oak—can act like a guillotine. I once saw a beaver caught on the ice hold off a pack of brush wolves, wounding several and I think killing one that went off to die—at least judging by the blood trail.

And I could not stop the dogs. It was nearly a half a mile to the beaver and while my attempts did slow the sledge somewhat we still made good time. I threw my weight sideways and flipped the sledge on its side, thinking it might help, but even that did nothing. Considering the work sledge was moving at nearly fifteen miles an hour and weighed close to four hundred pounds, plus another two with me on it, and judging the dogs' interest in the beaver by their pulling enthusiasm, the situation was fast approaching a critical stage.

I had one option left. Though I had stopped hunting and trapping and killing, I still carried a gun on the sledge. This for emergencies. I had been attacked by packs of feral dogs—both the team and me personally—so many times and with such great damage that I had decided to carry a handgun in case it happened again. So far it hadn't, but the handgun was there—a .357 magnum—and I could, in the end, possibly kill the beaver.

It certainly was not something I wanted to do, and in any event it was not all sure that I *could* do. I would have to fire the handgun from a bumping, moving sledge and try to hit a moving target before the dogs piled into it, which would ruin a clear shot. Taking into account that on a good day, holding the gun with both hands and standing rock-still, I could just about hit the side of a freight car, the whole thing really became academic.

But it was the last hope and I threw my right mitten off to let it hang on the cord and fumbled around sideways for the gun where it was tucked down inside the cargo bed of the sledge under a folded-over piece of tarp.

Again, the random patterns kicked in. Had I been able to, it's possible—not probable but possible—that I would have killed the beaver, rather than let him tear the team to pieces.

But I did it wrong. Or right.

I decided I would not be able to hit the beaver from the moving sledge so I worked out a plan. As the dogs grew closer, at the critical moment I would jump off the sledge and stand still and try to get a shot in before the dogs got too close for shooting and there would be risk of hitting them instead of the beaver. (Had this worked I would have had to walk the thirty or so miles home; the dogs were terrified of guns and the sudden shot would have scared them, made them run home without me.)

But once more the variables kicked in.

It started to go as planned. I watched them drag the sledge—still on its side—across the lake with me sitting on top of it, holding the gun, aimed like an arrow at the trundling beaver.

As we approached the beaver they picked up speed and I figured if I was lucky and everything went perfectly I would have just enough time for one shot; one carefully aimed, two-handed shot.

I poised, waiting for the right instant, the gun in one hand, the other on the sledge—the dogs moved, the sledge moved, and it was time. The exact moment.

I leaped.

And fell flat on my face. My foot hung up in a small crack in the surface of the ice and dumped me and I watched the gun go skittering across the snow in front of me. I scrabbled to my hands and knees and went after it, lunged, grabbed it, raised up on my knees and aimed, cocked the hammer . . .

Too late. The dogs had swerved, blocking any shot I might have had, and even when I jumped all the way up to my feet I couldn't see the beaver for the dogs.

I ran forward, expecting any second to hear the screams and growls of a full-fledged battle. The sled dogs had eaten many beaver—carcasses brought to me by trappers—and they would know what he was, how he tasted. I tried to run, kept falling on the slippery ice. They would not be able to stop themselves, would tear into him . . .

But I was wrong.

When I ran up and could see over the dogs and raised the gun in case a shot presented itself, nothing was as I predicted.

The beaver was there, sitting up on his back legs, his two-inch teeth exposed, making a low kind of chuttering sound in threat, ready for the attack.

But the dogs weren't attacking. They had come close to him, four, five feet away, and stopped and were sitting in a half circle, harnesses loose, ropes and tugs hanging, the sledge lying on its side in back of them.

They were studying him.

With the gun still raised, I moved forward and could now have shot and may have been able to hit him but it clearly wasn't necessary any longer and it suddenly struck me that they had never seen a beaver.

They had eaten them—chopped-up pieces of carcasses. Their jaws and teeth are so strong they even broke up the skulls and chewed at the beaver teeth.

But they had never seen a whole beaver, sitting there challenging them to do battle, and clearly some of the dogs couldn't believe it, and didn't seem to understand why this big, round, brown animal was so pissed off. So they sat in a half circle around him, studying him, looking at each other as if to shrug their shoulders, and when I walked up the beaver looked at me, the dogs, spat one last bit of defiance, turned and walked away across the lake, looking now and then over his shoulder at the team and me.

The dogs sat and watched him go, looked back at me, then lined out and untangled themselves—they had been running trapline and knew how to do such things—and we swung away from the beaver track and started off on our own way.

Every once in a while one or more of them would look back to the left to see how the beaver was doing as we trotted along, but they didn't pull off again or go after him. They just wanted to know what it was, walking across the ice on a cold January afternoon. Now they'd found out and it was time to go back to work. They were satisfied.

We ran those three lakes all of that day we saw the beaver and that night I stopped in a wonderful stand of Norway pines to camp. Later, while running and training Iditarod dogs there was never really time to camp— there was too much work to do. But at this stage I still stopped for the night and set up camp. It took me a few minutes to picket the dogs to small trees on individual cable leashes. Then I made a fire and started bringing in the massive amounts of wood it seemed to take to get through a forty-below night. With the wood stacked I flipped the sledge to clean off the loose snow, put it back upright, and arranged my sleeping bag and the foam pads in the sledge bed for the night.

It was by this time completely dark and I had not yet started to use a headlamp, so the only light was from the fire. Each dog had made a bed, scratching down through the snow to the grass beneath and then digging up the grass to make it fluffy and warm. I fed them chunks of meat, heated and softened by placing them in the snow around the fire, and then settled in for the night.

I didn't sleep well. It was far too beautiful. It had

been cloudy but the sky cleared and the moon was nearly full so the snow caught the light and filled the woods with pale images. I dozed in and out and when I would awaken everything would be different with the moon's movement. Trees changed, became standing figures, weeping nuns, slithering ghosts, flying dreams.

At two or three in the morning I was awakened for the fourth or fifth time by sound. I opened my eyes but heard nothing and was going to roll over and go back to sleep when I decided I should at least check the dogs. I sat up and looked over the side of the sled and found them all to be standing in the moonlight. This was not so unusual—they frequently stood and turned when they slept to make a new position or remake their beds. I had one dog named Fonzi who would spend hours each night remaking his bed and he never got it quite right.

I watched them for a moment, saw that some of them were leaning toward each other, pulling at their cable leashes. But they were wagging their tails and not growling or acting aggressive so I did a quick head count, came up with nine, and lay back to resume sleep.

It didn't hit me for several minutes and when it did I almost didn't sit up. The temperature had dropped to a still forty below and the inside of the bag was warm and cozy. I closed my eyes, started to doze and even when it came to me I thought I was dreaming.

I only had eight dogs with me.

I sat up and counted again. Even in the bright moonlight some of the dogs were lost in shadows that seemed to move and I had to count carefully.

Nine dogs.

I squinted, watching the shapes. Each dog was tied to its own tree, saplings three or four inches thick, with a five-foot lead. The saplings were close together so that some of the dogs could overlap a nose or tail— all right for the dogs that didn't fight—but the whole picket area was partly shaded by tall Norway pines that put blob shapes of moon shadow over everything and made it hard to see.

All things seemed to check out. The dogs were all still tied, or appeared to be, there were no fights, they all seemed to be quiet—though up on their feet and interested in each other—and it would have been a normal night except that there were nine of them and I only had an eight-dog team.

There were still coals in the fire. I took a handful of kindling from the morning pile near the sled and dumped it on the coals, then added some sticks of pitch wood I'd found near a burned stump. In the flare from the pitch a yellow light brightened the whole clearing and I counted the dogs in real light instead of the ghost light from the moon.

Eight dogs.

Right, I thought. In the moonlight I've got nine dogs, in the firelight I'm back to eight.

By now any thought of sleep was gone. I had thoughts of ghost dogs, dream dogs, vision dogs—dogs I'd read about in books on ancient dog runners, before history knew of dog runners, back when they ran a rawhide collar around a dog's neck and didn't have harnesses.

I sat up in the sled, bundled in my bag but higher now so I could see better, and let the fire die down again, watching, waiting to see eight dogs turn into nine.

I almost missed it.

The light from the fire ruined night vision and as the flames died it came back slowly. I watched the shadows, counted and recounted the dogs, going back and forth with my eyes in steps and on the third sweep I saw it happen.

A shadow, no more than a subtle shape, separated from the other moon shadows. At first it seemed just another blob of darkness—my eyes were still ruined by the fire—but as it moved and went through a patch of moonlight between shadows I saw that it was a dog.

No. Not a dog.

A wolf.

It was much too small to be a timber wolf. Forty pounds, maybe a little more, with skinny legs and an extraordinary fluffed coat that made it seem like a fur pom-pom with legs, the "dog" was a brush wolf— northern coyote—and it went in with the dogs like it had been doing so all its life.

I waited for the barking, the screaming, the fights, and none of it came. The dogs greeted the newcomer like an old lost friend, wagging their tails and nuzzling, and I wondered again if I was dreaming. It was all so vague, so shadowy. The wolf would be there, then move and the shadows would slide and it would be gone. I would see nine dogs, then only four as the shadows moved, then eleven as they came back, and I sat in the moonlight like a mummy, the bag up around my ears and head so only my face showed and watched them all night—sleeping in and out—while they played and talked to the wolf.

When daylight came I had been dozing and I snapped awake in the gray dawn and saw that the wolf was gone. I lit a fire and heated tea and a can of beef stew and meat for the dogs.

When I fed there were nine of them again. The wolf had come back, didn't seem afraid of me, and ate meat when I threw a piece to it.

Or her. I had decided it was a female. She looked fine-boned and moved quickly, and to dispel any further doubt she was in season, she kept teasing and backing into the dogs to be bred after she'd eaten. While I was sipping tea the dogs went wild, barking and screaming, and I turned to see she had hung with a male named Typhoon and when they were solid I slipped my shoepacs on and moved closer to see her better. The dogs quieted once they were hung up and turned to watch me as I approached.

She pulled away slightly and bared her teeth when I was ten feet away so I moved off a bit and stood, studying her. She'd been trapped once. Her right front paw had been broken up and healed deformed. I had seen it before with dogs, my dogs. Some son of a bitch (I always thought of him that way) had actually set traps in my sled dog trail and I ran a team onto them. Only one dog got hit but it was a number four double spring and it broke his foot all to hell (it is complete bullshit that leghold traps don't hurt the animal), and he was out the season while a vet rebuilt his foot.

She didn't favor the paw and didn't seem concerned that I was around—just when I got too near—and she was beautiful in a way that only wild things can be beautiful. Her hair was a complete coat, so thick I doubt rain would have penetrated, and so even and clean it looked to be trimmed and coiffed by a beautician.

"Marge."

The name slipped out aloud. It was her eyes. They reminded me of a woman I'd known named Marge. Up at the outside corners and inquisitive. Her ears went up when I said it, but so did the other dogs'—it was a sudden sound and broke the cold silence.

She finished her business with Typhoon and pranced a bit out around the dogs the way they do when they've bred and they're feeling frisky.

She seemed so amiable and playful and unafraid that I felt I could pet her, get close to her, but if I moved toward her at all she moved away; never far, never running off but well out of reach.

It was amazing, considering the relationship between northern coyotes and humans in that region. They had killed hundreds, thousands of sheep, the small "wolves"—enough so that many people on the edge of the forest had to stop raising sheep. There was some controversy about it, but I had seen many cases where two or three of the coyotes would kill dozens of sheep in a single night, pulling an ear here, or ripping an udder there, not eating them but hurting the sheep enough so they would die. The upshot of all this was that people—especially farmers—shot the coyotes out of hand. Often they would hang the bodies on fences in the belief—erroneous—that the carcasses would keep other coyotes away.

The coyotes had learned of guns the hard way, and it was almost impossible to find one that didn't scoot the minute they saw a person, and keep moving until they were well out of range.

But Marge—as I came to think of her—stayed with us all that day and more, three days and nights. And in so doing showed me something I never would have seen, showed me the inside of a wild mind.

Dogs are . . . wonderful. Truly. To know them and be with them is an experience that transcends—a way to understand the joyfulness of living and devotion.

But they are dogs. They have been allied with man for thousands, perhaps hundreds of thousands of years. And while some of them are close to wild—Eskimo sled dogs, some old village breeds—they are still linked to man, still have that connection to humans that makes them not truly wild. Love, food, life, direction, all come from humans to the dogs, and it affects the way they are, the way they can be seen.

Wild things—wolves, bear, coyotes—all have a way of life that takes man into consideration, especially when it concerns fear of death, but they do not value man as part of their living equation. (There are some exceptions of course—bears and city dumps are the best example—but as a rule wild things live alone, adjacent to man, perhaps, but not *of* man.)

Because of this separation from the wild it is almost impossible to see wild thinking, to be part of a truly wild life.

That morning I harnessed with Marge watching, sitting out to the side quietly. The dogs were interested in her still, but not overly, and did not try to go to her or run with her.

When they were harnessed and the sled was loaded and ready I lined them out and jerked the hook and we started off. The trail we ran was packed because we'd been over it so many times, but off to the side it was still deep powder. Marge was fast and light on her feet and very agile, but she could not keep up with the team—they were running full out and fresh—in the deep powder. But as soon as we moved out of the camp area and onto the hard-packed trail, she dropped in to our rear and had no trouble keeping up with us.

I do not know why she followed us. I had theories: she was a coyote somebody raised from a pup and was accustomed to being with people, Typhoon was so important to her she wanted to mate again, she wanted more easy food . . .

There was no way to know. But she did. Mile after mile, running with us, just thirty, forty yards back. When I'd stop to snack the dogs I'd throw her a piece of meat and she'd snap it up. If we stopped to look at a view or watch a deer or a moose she would stop and watch as well.

❊ ❊ ❊

I was not going to go home.

It was neither a concrete decision nor a sudden one—more a gradual realization, a dawning of some new part of my life I didn't quite understand but knew

I had to do. I had plenty of food riding in the sled for the dogs and more for myself. Ruth would worry some if I was late, but I had been late before when trapping and it had worked out all right. And that had been when it was more dangerous, working around beaver lodges on bad ice or setting the large Conibear 330 double-spring instant-kill traps that could break an arm if caution wasn't used.

Now I was just running dogs and she would know it was safer and not worry. (It was a wrong assumption: by the second day she had people out looking for me thinking I'd gone through the ice or broken a leg. I pointed out that things like that never happened to me, which proved incorrect as well: within a year and a half I would do both.)

What I wanted to see, to feel, to be was *not* at home. It was out here in the winter woods running these dogs. So I turned north and started watching the horizon, started trying to see over the next hill, started hoping and waiting for some new grand thing to come around the next bend—began, in other words, to do those things that would lead inevitably to the Iditarod, though I did not know it then.

The dogs sensed something was different as well. We ran across a lake where we had always run— Marge still trotting along in back of us—and at the end of the lake where the river flowed out there was a patch of water that stayed open year round because the water flowed so rapidly.

Steam boiled up from the open water and I always ran there because there were usually new tracks

around the open patch where animals came to hunt—
or play. I had seen otter there twice, sliding down the
banks into the water.

But we had always turned left there, near the
open water, and moved back along the edge of the
lake and headed in the direction of home.

This time we stopped there, watching. When there
were no otters (I found later they had been trapped—
though it was not legal to trap them and the pelts could
not be sold legally) I called the dogs up and gave the
command for a right turn.

"Gee." *Haw* was the command for left.

I was running a dog named Cookie for a leader
then. She had become more than a dog, more than a
friend—almost an alter ego—in the year of trapping
and work. And she was so sure I was mistaken she
started to take the dogs left and home.

"Gee," I repeated, and she stopped then and looked
back over the dogs at me, to make sure.

Yes, I nodded. "Gee."

She snapped around to the right and started up the
side of the lakeshore. As soon as she'd moved a few
feet and was clear of the water I called again. "Now
haw—straight ahead."

It confused her but only for a moment. She looked
back once more to make certain I hadn't lost my mind
and then jumped gleefully ahead, out around the water
along an ice ledge wide enough for the dogs and sled
and down the river.

I had once glanced at a map of this river. It was
narrow—not more than twenty yards wide at the widest and usually more like twenty or thirty feet—and

shallow. But it meandered all over for miles and miles in a generally northwesterly direction.

After that I didn't know anything about it. Not where it ended, nor if that point could be reached with a dog team. And I didn't care. I let them go, ran without talking to them and a strange thing happened.

They, we, all the dogs and I wanted to know was what came next. The river wound back and forth, sometimes covering half a mile of winding to make a hundred yards in a straight-line direction.

As the dogs approached each bend they would swing out to see around the bend, to see what was coming next, and I found myself doing the same thing. I would lean over on the sled, out to the side to see around the turn, waiting. Waiting.

I had forgotten Marge and on one of the turns she went past me on the left at a quick, darting lope and moved out in front of the team. They couldn't stand that and picked up the pace to catch her and for a mile or so I had a wild ride, careening down the packed ice of the wide-open river, whipping on the turns, until Marge suddenly jumped up the bank on the right and disappeared over the top.

The dogs tried to follow her and started to fall back—the bank was steep—until Cookie clawed at the edge and pulled them over. I hung on the sled for a moment, then bounced up in back of them.

The river had been winding through hardwood forests, bare of leaves, of course, but thickly set like thousands of fingers aimed at the sky. But here the terrain had changed, become more hilly, and the river was

cutting through thick pines and spruce with old poplars lying blown and dead.

It was impossible to get a team or sled through the
tangled mess so I hit the brakes and set the hook on a
tree and started to go up and pull Cookie around to get
them back down on the river.

But Marge hadn't gone far. She had stopped
twenty or twenty-five yards in front of Cookie and
was standing, her head cocked, ignoring the dogs.
They had whined a bit but were silent now, watching the coyote, and I waited with my hand on the
X of Cookie's harness where it crossed on her back,
watching Marge.

She had something specific in mind. She had followed us for miles on the river, trotting along in back
of the dogs, and then suddenly zoomed past to get to
this place ahead of us.

I could not see anything special in the woods. The
pines were second or third growth—not terribly
large—and the poplars had fallen from the wind and
turned the grove into a tangle that would take decades
to rot down to mulch.

In the middle there were several small clearings. It
was still early—not yet two in the afternoon—but the
sun was low and there was a feeling of dusk in the air.
I studied the clearings, could see nothing, then noted
Marge and the way she was looking and tried again.
On the third attempt I saw it.

There were small disturbances in the powder snow
in the clearings, almost riffles, and by squatting down
I could see little jets of steam coming from the disturbances. They were grouse burrows.

It had been cold the night before and would be cold again this night. When the snow is soft and powdery grouse jump from a tree limb and "fly" down in a straight line to burrow into the snow to make little caves to stay warm. The steam I saw was their breath coming up from the burrows.

Marge had known these grouse were here, or were likely to be here, and had come ahead to get dinner. I had seen dogs do similiar things, remember places they had seen only once, remember every aspect, every stick, every shape after passing through a place only once, and I thought this must be a place Marge was familiar with. She probably passed through here once a week or so on her regular circuit.

But she did not have the grouse yet. It was one thing to see them and something else to get one of them. I had skied up quite close to their burrows when hunting and sometimes been almost on top of them. But they sense vibration and hear incredibly well in the cold silence and I knew Marge would probably not get close to the burrows before they exploded out.

I made certain of the hook holding on the tree. There were many high-bush cranberries about with the berries frozen on the limbs, a favorite grouse winter food. There might be three or four of them in the snow, and when Marge scared them and they blew out the dogs would go crazy and try to chase them. I didn't want the team and sled and me to get tangled up in that mess of deadfalls and limbs.

I needn't have worried. Marge knew exactly what she was doing.

She studied the clearing carefully for another minute or so, seemed to be looking at each tree, and I didn't understand it until suddenly she jumped, in a springy, light-footed leap that took her well clear of the snow—at least six feet in the air—and she landed on a deadfall.

The deadfall was a poplar about ten inches in diameter that had broken off halfway up in a strong wind two or three years earlier. It had dried, not rotted, and angled down to where it had hung up in another poplar five or so feet off the ground with the high end up at fifteen feet or so, caught on the stump.

Marge landed on the low end of the deadfall, paused to get her balance, then deftly trotted up the deadfall to the high end. This put her fifteen feet off the ground, and perhaps another fifteen feet off to the side of the grouse.

Here she paused again, looking at the burrows in the snow. I knew what she was studying. The grouse do not go in straight but angle off to make an igloo kind of entrance to the burrow so they won't lose heat. The place where the entry hole is located might be a foot and a half or two feet from where the grouse was actually sitting and she wanted to make certain she located the grouse and not just the hole.

The dogs had been sitting through part of this, but when she jumped up on the deadfall they stood and some of them whined softly in excitement.

She tensed and then leapt, in the same high arc above where she was standing, so that she might have been sixteen or eighteen feet in the air. Then she plummeted into the snow like an arrow, head and feet first, mouth open.

The world exploded. She came up at once with a flapping grouse in her mouth, but at the same time four or five others—it was hard to count them—blew out of the snow like bombs going off, carrying a spray of powdery white twenty feet in the air.

I had been standing on the sled and the dogs went mad and jerked against the hook, which in turn jerked the sled and dropped me hind end first in the snow.

It took ten minutes to sort the dogs out again. They had jumped over each other and were all tangled. And I was back down on the river with the team heading northwest before I realized exactly all that I had seen.

Marge ate the grouse in what seemed moments, pulling the body out of the feathers and swallowing it almost whole before following us again.

But it was the act of hunting that dazzled me, had me wondering about fundamental values. She had used tools. Chimps use them, make and use crude tools to eat termites, and gorillas have done the same to make beds, but the incredible chauvinism of the human species has demanded that we make differences. It probably has to do with the biblical silliness about the humans having dominion over the earth, but we always seem to try and elevate ourselves above others—within the species as well as without. One of the separation methods has been the use of reason and the use of tools. Humans, these people would say, can reason and use tools to achieve their end. Other species cannot.

Marge did both. She reasoned in a very complicated manner—one which few people would perhaps think to do. She found the grouse by knowing where they would be, then also knew she couldn't get close to them without using some exterior device—tool—to help her.

We ran four more days and for three of those days she ran with us. I fed her from the dog food I had brought but she clearly didn't need it. She trotted along in back of us as we ran the river, taking a side trip when she was hungry. Twice more she took grouse, and three times snowshoe rabbit—each time bounding off the trail into the deeper snow, then coming back out with food hanging in her mouth.

She bred twice more with Typhoon—staying selective—and I hoped that when I at last started home she would follow and stay around the cabin to have her pups, but it was not to be. On the third day we crossed a medium-sized lake. It was quiet and clear and cold but the sun was warm where it hit my face. I still had no direction, no thought of where to go, and let the dogs head across the lake on their own, Cookie picking her own way.

As we started Marge followed, but halfway across the lake I looked back and she had turned off to the side, trotting away at a ninety-degree angle to our direction.

I stopped the dogs and called to her.

"Hey—where're you going?"

Stupid, I thought. But she stopped and looked at me, forty, fifty yards away, seemed to study me for a moment, then turned her shoulders back in something close to a shrug and trotted on. I watched her move the rest of the way across that lake and jump up on the bank and disappear in the brush and all the way I felt like I was losing a friend. For the rest of the time I trained there and ran through the same area, I watched for her and hoped to see her but never did; nor did I hear of a trapper or anybody shooting her. She was there and gone—a small wonder.

The remainder of that first long run was full of small wonders, little miracles. They were not things to move mountains, but events to alter my mind, the way I thought; events to lead me ultimately and perhaps inevitably to the Iditarod.

A chickadee stayed on the rim of my parka hood for half a day, sitting there like a hood ornament even when I fed the dogs, taking bits of meat from my finger and peeking back down over the top of the hood at my face while I was riding the sled through the woods.

We came upon a snared deer on the fourth day. In times past it was a method of taking deer. Men would use steel cable snares set over deer trails with tin cans or bits of iron tied to the cables. When a deer hit it and felt the snare tightening around its neck it would panic and thrash, strangling itself to death. The tin cans and bits of metal clanging served two purposes: to make the deer go crazy and panic and to signal the trapper if his cabin wasn't too far away that he had snared a deer.

Snaring deer is strictly illegal but snares are still used legally for brush wolves and fox. The size of cable is closely controlled so that no cable is allowed that would hold a deer or large animal; also the snares are to be kept low so that a deer would not naturally stick its head through it.

Supposedly.

But trappers are men and make the same mistakes other men do. I had seen horrible things done to animals by trappers quite by accident. I found a fox that had been dead for well over a year—nothing left but a skeleton with a bony paw still in a leg-hold trap. The fox had gone around and around so long before dying of thirst that he had worn a groove a foot deep around the trap stake and the skeleton lay pointed out, somehow undisturbed by scavengers, as if still trying to get away. (I found later that this particular trapper—his name was on the trap and I turned it in to the authorities—was a drunk and frequently set traps and then forgot where he set them and never went back to check them and left animals hanging in them regularly.)

A similiar thing happened with the snared deer. A trapper had used a full quarter-inch cable—strong enough to pull a car—for the snare, and made the loop much too big and then compounded the error by tying it off to a six-inch-thick tree that was too high off the ground for coyotes. To be sure, a deer moving with its head held well up could probably have missed it or brushed it aside on a shoulder and been all right. But deer often walk along with their head down, smelling the ground, browsing on bits of willow, especially in the winter.

And so this doe had done. She had come on this snare while her head was down, taken a step and put her head through it, and probably when the cable had brushed her ears she had jerked back and tightened it.

These snares are equipped with a noose-locking mechanism that will only allow them to tighten, never loosen, and as the animal struggles the snare draws up tighter and tighter until the animal chokes to death. The more the animal fights the worse it is and the quicker it dies. But at first, when it first hits, the fear tears at them and they go insane trying to get away.

The doe had acted normally. In the first moments she had gone crazy, pulling and running around the tree, back and forth, tearing at the brush until she'd cleared a circle all around the snare tree.

Normally death would have come then. But as the doe had hit the brush in some way a piece of wood a foot or so long and wrist thick had become wedged under the cable against her throat and had prevented the cable from clamping down tightly on her windpipe.

It had tightened, and cut her air, and she was all but unconscious but she still lived. Yet at first, when we came on her next to the river, I thought she was dead. She had gone around the tree several times at the last, wrapping the cable and shortening it until her neck was pinched against the tree and she was hanging, her head three feet off the ground, her body inert.

The riverbank was seven or eight feet high at this point, and she was back up over the lip in such a way that the dogs couldn't see her while I could because of my greater height.

I knew immediately what had happened and thought I would go up and at least take the meat to feed to the dogs so it wouldn't go to waste. The trapper would just have dragged her off and left her somewhere since it was illegal and he would not want attention.

I tied the sled off to a tree and then fastened another rope from Cookie's harness to a tree ahead of her to hold the team tight and keep them from following me.

In the sled I had a pair of combination pliers/wire cutters and I took them and climbed the bank to cut the cable and dress her out.

She was so far gone I did not realize until I had the cutters jammed through the cable by her neck that life still remained, though it was not much of a life. I cut the cable at once and eased her head down. The snow was deep and I had been kneeling next to what I thought was a body so that when her head came down it fell naturally into my lap.

I still did not think she would live and I was enraged that she would have suffered so. The cable had cut into her hide and left a line around her neck where it wore the hair off and in my anger I kept trying to rub the line out, straighten the hair, make up for what had happened to her. It just seemed such a waste—in some way like killing children, very sweet children, to kill deer this way, or any way—and I found myself rubbing harder and harder until suddenly I saw a change come into her eyes.

Her head was still in my lap and her eyes had been partially glazed—I thought in coma or nearing death—but a look came in them now, a look of interest, and they widened in fear.

There was a second when it could have gone either way. Deer have amazingly sharp hooves and as a matter of fact they can kill. I saw a doe once kill a brush wolf with one stab of her front feet and a child was killed at a state park by an overly friendly "pet" deer that jumped on him.

I was kneeling in the snow petting a wild deer who at any split second could explode in my face. The problem was I could not move away without throwing myself backwards, which would cause her to panic and lash out, and if I stayed I wasn't sure how she would handle it.

So I sat, and without thinking my hand was still petting her neck where the snare had cut.

She stared up at me without moving, and I have read since that in predator-prey relationships there comes a point where the prey goes into shock and becomes still while it is killed. Later, much later, many times later I thought of that and wondered if she was in shock and so remained still.

But she didn't seem to be. She looked into my eyes and then rolled her own eyes down to see my hand on her neck. She looked back up at me and started to get up and then lay back down, putting the weight of her neck on my legs while I kept petting her.

Presently—a few minutes, a half-hour, a day; I could not think in terms of time—she raised her head slowly and got her legs beneath her and stood. As she rose the dogs saw her and barked and jerked to get loose and she started a bit when they made noise.

But she didn't run. She stood three or four feet away from me, breathing deeply, watching me, and then turned and walked away, twice looking back over her shoulder at me before disappearing beneath an overhanging balsam limb.

❋ ❋ ❋

I was on the run again, working the team along the river, when I started to think of them—the doe and Marge—not as something in the wild, something to be observed, but as good friends that I had come to know and understand.

It was in some way a fundamental change in how I perceived myself and the world. I did not elevate myself any longer, nor did I put the other aspects of nature down. It became, truly, we.

When I came off the run—had been living in beauty for those days and nights, had seen and done those things that so basically altered me—I stopped the dogs in the kennel and put them on their chains and could not think of it ending.

I made food and fed them and brought them all new straw for their houses and then sat on Cookie's house and looked at our cabin.

It was dark. We had run all that day to get home and had come in silently. This was before we had many dogs and since I was running all the dogs we owned, there were none to bark and alert the house when we came in.

The dogs made their beds, stirred the straw around to fluff it up, and then grew quiet. Somewhere a mile or more away a brush wolf howled, a soft cut through the still night. The sound was faint but awakened two of the dogs and they raised their heads and whined softly and I knew, *knew* what the whine meant, knew that it meant they would answer the howl but they were tired and full of food and the straw was warm and to hell with it.

I do not honestly think that I could have gone into the house then and perhaps never, never into the house again. I did not belong there any longer. The run, the dogs, knowing the dogs and how they felt, how I had become part of them.

I just could not go into the house, and I sat on top of Cookie's house and maybe would have continued to sit there all night, all my life, except that the door on the cabin opened and Ruth came outside with a pan of dirty water. She threw it on the stalagmite of frozen dishwater next to the door—an art form we worked at—and looked up to the kennel and saw me sitting there looking toward the house.

She went inside and came out a minute later with a parka on, holding a steaming cup. I watched her walk to the kennel in silence. She stopped and handed me the cup and I found it was hot soup. I sipped it and it was delicious—better than anything I had ever tasted.

"I was worried," she said after a bit. "I sent Ray on a snowmachine to find you but he lost your tracks up north, by Clearwater Lake . . ."

"I'm sorry. I was just running them. Running the dogs." I swallowed more soup and looked at the sky. The cold air was so clear the stars seemed to be falling to the ground. Like you could walk right . . . over . . . there and pick them up just lying on the snow. "I couldn't come back."

She said nothing for another minute or so, then sighed. "You're different. About the dogs, I mean. Somehow you've changed."

"Yes." A feeling of profound knowledge seemed to take me—or of profound ignorance. A lack of knowing and a desire to know. "I *am* different. I see things the way they see them."

"Who sees them?"

"The dogs." And then the thought: *the other dogs.* "They see it all the time."

"You're going to run the race, aren't you?"

"What race?" And as god is a witness I meant it— I was not thinking of any race. Just the sweep of running them, the incredible joy of it all.

"That one up in Alaska."

"The Iditarod?"

"Yes. That one. You're going to go do it, aren't you?"

We had spoken of the Iditarod a few times. Had heard of it and wondered at the insanity of it, how mad it was to run it. One relative actually told me, "Real people don't do that kind of thing," and I had agreed with her. I had, at most, run a dog team 150 or so miles over a four-day period, wandering happily, slowly, stopping to camp. I knew nothing of Alaska, crossing mountain ranges, running on sea ice, racing with a team over 1,000 miles, 1,100 miles of wilderness, 1,180 miles of snow and deep cold, cold like I had never even imagined, winds beyond belief, roaring waters and deadly dreams—a world, a whole world beyond my knowing. Right then I was probably one of the least qualified dog drivers on the entire planet to go up and run the Iditarod.

"Yes," I answered, listening to Cookie breathe in the silence of Ruth waiting. "I think I am . . ."

Dogs from Hell

The dogs stood in the middle of the yard and stared at me as if in question, and in truth there was much room for their asking.

They were three dogs from Canada—Devil, Ortho, and Murphy—and had worked a Canadian trapline since they were pups four years earlier. Wild, rangy dogs used to traveling long distances. As with Cookie and the rest, they were no specific breed, but various mixes of pulling dogs—with a dollop of wolf thrown in. My wife and I had driven up to Canada in an old borrowed pickup with a camper shell to buy them and brought them back in three plastic dog kennels bought at the local pet store. Or tried to bring them back. The truth is there is an enormous disparity between what pet store owners think might be a sled dog and what actually *is* a sled dog. The kennels were clearly designed for a fantasy dog that simply sat and accepted what was happening to him and wasn't concerned with freedom. Or maybe a poodle. They had *not* been designed for three Eskimo village dogs with jaws like sharks.

Devil and Ortho shredded their kennels before we'd gone five miles. It was just a fluke that I caught it. As I pulled to a stop at a stop sign before turning onto a highway, I heard a growling sound and thought the rear end of the pickup was going out. I opened the door to look underneath the truck and happened to glance inside the camper shell and saw that Devil had his head sticking out the side of his kennel, a wild look in his marbled-blue-and-brown eyes, teeth bared and snarling at me. While I watched he seemed to shrug and the kennel fell away from him. Ortho had gone one better and completely dismembered his kennel and was loose inside the camper shell and working at eating through the plastic and aluminum side windows. Murphy wasn't chewing—I would find later he wasn't too smart—but sat in his kennel howling, deep, mournful howl-growls that I had heard and mistaken for mechanical troubles.

"What are we going to do?" My wife had gotten out of the truck as well and stood looking in at the dogs the way she might view a couple of serial killers. "We have two hundred miles to go . . ."

"One of us," I tried hopefully, "will have to ride back here with them and keep them in."

"You're the one who wants to run the Iditarod," she said firmly. "I'll drive the truck."

"I understand." I moved to the rear of the truck and stopped with my hand on the camper door handle.

"It will give you a chance to learn about the dogs, get acquainted with them."

I nodded. I had never touched them. The man who sold them to us loaded them in the kennels. "Yes, that too—I'll get to know them." But I still did not turn the handle. The growl-howl from inside the camper was deafening. It sounded like somebody was being torn apart.

The killer sentence. "You *wanted* to do this."

"I know."

"So . . ."

Feeling like I was about to throw myself on top of a grenade I turned the handle, opened the door a crack, and slithered in before any dogs could get out.

For a moment nothing happened. Murphy kept howling from inside his kennel but Devil and Ortho just stared at me, probably stunned that they would be given such an incredible opportunity. That anybody would be stupid enough to get into a small, confined space with the two of them at the same time was simply unbelievable. A dream come true.

"See?" My wife was watching through the side window. "They *like* you—it's going to be just fine . . ."

She turned away to get into the truck and the moment her face left the window Ortho and Devil hit me chest high and I went over and backwards and down with two dogs in my face.

I remember feeling the truck lurch as Ruth put it in gear and started out onto the highway and thinking critically—and somewhat pompously—that she still hadn't learned to use the clutch right and then everything was pandemonium.

It was never quite clear after that just exactly what was happening or who was on top and who on the bottom or who was biting or being bitten.

I know at one point all lofty thoughts of running dogs and Iditarods and the dance with winter were gone and I was thinking that if I could just get out of the camper shell alive and with most of my extremities I would be satisfied.

One of the problems lay in the fact that Ortho and Devil had a serious personality conflict going of which I was unaware.

First they chewed at the camper shell but when I pulled them back from that they went for each other and when I tried to hold them apart by their collars they looked at me quizzically and with great glee tried to eat my arms, or legs, or whatever they could get. So I would let them go and they would tear at each other and then at me . . .

And so it went for three hours without a letup.

By the time we arrived home I was on full autopilot, had lost enough blood to save a hemophiliac, and had actually started to growl and bite back when they bit me. Somehow we got them on chains in the kennel and went into the house where Ruth helped me go through thirty or so gallons of hydrogen peroxide and a couple of miles of tape and bandage.

"The men at the customs gate were so funny," she said. "They looked inside the camper shell and asked which one was the human. I laughed for miles and miles."

"It wasn't funny."

"Oh yes, dear. It was very funny. It may have hurt, but it was still very funny." And she walked out of the house laughing and shaking her head while I stood dripping blood and peroxide on the floor.

And now here they stood—the three of them, Ortho, Murphy, and Devil—tied to the picket line waiting for me to do something.

The truth was I didn't know what to do and it showed . . .

Ortho scratched at an ear, lifted his leg, and pissed on Murphy. Devil—keeping his eyes directly on my face, in my eyes (not a good sign; direct eye-contact is a threat)—leaned across Ortho and pissed on Murphy. Murphy didn't seem to mind.

Ruth was standing by the front door of the house watching me and the dogs.

"They remind me of that time when you were drunk and you brought the bikers home to dinner . . ."

"I thought we were never going to talk about that again."

"They're kind of the same. Cuter, though."

"The bikers?"

"The dogs. But they pee on each other the same way."

I still didn't know what to do. It was an early fall day—late summer, really—and these dogs were my first attempt at putting together a team to run the Iditarod.

When I had decided—or realized that the decision had been made for me in some way by the dogs—to run the race, I had bumped smack into the fundamental problem that comes to all who run it.

Dogs.

It is really not a sled race, nor a race of people—though many people take credit for it—nor of money (though that is a close second ingredient), nor of macho idiocy nor of feminine strength nor intellect nor bravery . . .

It is a dog race.

And the primary ingredient, the base of the equation, is dogs.

It takes a quantity of dogs and they must be dogs of sufficient quality so they can make the run without hurting themselves. Such dogs, in a world mad with dogs, are exceedingly rare.

I had a trapline team, that is, a work team, of seven dogs with one excellent leader and dear friend named Cookie. They were good dogs and I loved them—and still love them—but there is a large difference between running twenty or thirty miles a day on a trapline or hauling in a load of firewood now and then and running a hundred miles a day through mountains taller than the Rockies.

I needed dogs.

I called everybody I could find who lived in the lower forty-eight states who had ever run the Iditarod—two men—and asked them what to do.

"About what?" one of them asked.

"About everything." I was so ignorant I didn't

even know the questions, let alone the answers. "The race. Dogs. Sleds. Clothes. Food. Everything."

"Wear mukluks." Click.

I turned to Ruth. "What the hell are mukluks?"

"They're a kind of footgear," she said. "I just read about them. They're supposed to be very warm."

The other man was slightly less terse.

"You have to have good dogs. Try to get good dogs . . ."

"Where?"

Click.

And so the search began.

I had seven dogs. In my innocence—or, as Ruth put it, idiocy—I did some simple math. I read that most people ran fifteen or sixteen dogs. I only needed eight or nine more.

"How hard can it be," I asked Ruth, "to find eight or nine dogs?"

I somehow thought that you just came up with the right number of dogs and ran the race and that it all worked out somehow. I didn't think in terms of extra dogs in case of injuries from fighting or moose attacks or drunks on snowmachines (and why is it all snow-machine drivers seem to be drunk?) or idiotic deer hunters who shoot into kennels or viruses or sex rearing its ugly head or dog headaches or just dog moods. Some days they don't want to run and there is nothing you can do to get them to run.

All in all it can be damn hard to find eight or nine dogs that could run the Iditarod. (I was to read later—when I needed it most—of a man who ran the Iditarod his first time with virtually no dogs to start with; he went to the Anchorage dog pound and took just about everything they had. But he found that none of them would lead, so he tied a rope around his waist and left the starting chutes running as the lead dog himself. He finished dead last—I think in twenty-eight days—but it is probably still the greatest run in the history of the race.)

It can be hard to find even *one* dog that can run the Iditarod.

I started calling dog people, sprint kennels that had extra dogs, old dogs, tired dogs, dogs that were too slow for the shorter sprint races where they run wide open for seven or eight miles and are then put to bed.

They came in dribs and drabs. A dog here, a dog there—many times it was just people unloading their worst dogs. Sometimes it was people who meant well but who—like myself—simply didn't understand the enormity of the Iditarod.

Sweet dogs, sour dogs, dogs that wagged and bit at the same time, dogs that wouldn't be happy unless they had a finger to eat, dogs that just lay down and looked at you when you harnessed them, dogs that loved to run, hated to run, dogs that made war, dogs that gave up and some, rare ones, who never, ever did.

Dogs like people.

And then the dogs from Canada . . .

True northern sled dogs like Devil, Ortho, and Murphy. Huge, gray-sided, yellow-eyed meat eaters that didn't want anything but to pull and eat; no petting, no love, no hate, no touch. Just a harness and a horizon.

They stood, watching me. Or Devil and Ortho stood. Murphy sat in what I would learn was a perpetual near-coma state.

I had been doing some reading. Dog mushing pamphlets, an old army field manual titled something like *Transportation, Dog Team, One Each* (which, all joking aside, would prove to be invaluable), pictures in magazines.

I knew that sprint racers trained in the summer and fall, before snow, with what they called "rigs"— homemade wheeled outfits the dogs could pull. I did not have such a rig yet to run the dogs with, and since there was no snow I had no real way of testing them, even for a short run. Or thought I hadn't.

"We have that old bicycle," Ruth said. "The one you got at that auction for $1.25 . . ."

"I thought we weren't going to talk about that, either."

I go crazy at auctions. Not only did I buy the bicycle but a bobsled—the kind that was used for hauling logs in the old logging camps—for $2.50 (only to find out it weighed seven hundred pounds and I couldn't get it home) and nineteen adult geese for three dollars more. I did get the geese home; they leveled the garden, covered everything in a three-inch layer of goose crap, and killed one of Ruth's cats before I could find somebody kind enough to take them off my hands.

"I just thought the bicycle might work. You could hook Cookie up and one or two of the others with a long rope . . ."

I should have listened to her. She was reason, logic, sensibility.

But I sometimes extrapolated too soon with things and before she finished explaining how it might be used, I was gone and had fetched the bike—an old, fat-tired Schwinn. I took the gangline off the sled and hooked it to the front of the bike, tied a safety line off to a tree with the bike lying on the ground, and started getting dogs.

I hooked Cookie up in front, then a dog named Max on point—the position just in back of the leader—and then Ortho, Murphy, and Devil. Ortho came willingly and Murphy slumped on down but Devil took chunks out of me and reminded me of old cartoons with the Tasmanian devil in them; he snarled and snapped and bit at anything that was close.

"Don't you think you might have rather more dogs than you need?" Ruth asked, watching from the side.

"Naww—it'll be fine."

I picked the bike up. It was slightly off to the side, the dogs and the gangline pulling on the rope tied to the tree past the bike.

As soon as I moved to the bike Cookie stood and took up the slack and the rest of them started slamming into their harnesses and screaming in high, piercing yelps.

I sat on the bike, balanced it and lined it up with the direction the dogs would be pulling and reached my hand toward the mechanical quick release that would slide up and let the rope loose.

Some instinct, a genetic will to live intervened and I hesitated. The rope leading up into the gangline was trembling, quivering like the string on a guitar. I put my finger on it and pulled back instantly. It fairly hummed and I realized that there was enormous power there—more power than I had ever felt on the sled with my regular team—and it was fewer dogs than I normally ran.

"I don't know," I started to say to Ruth. "Maybe I ought to leave a dog or two home . . ."

The rope holding the gangline to the tree broke at that instant and the bike shot out of the yard, heading for the road at what seemed terminal velocity.

I wobbled once, regained balance, and managed through my terror to achieve some small amount of control. The trees in the yard went by in a mad blur, and I felt the end of the driveway approaching at warp speed.

Cookie was in full glory. There had been dogs behind her before, the trapping dogs, but this was different—these dogs were powerful, driving.

At the end of the driveway I yelled, "Gee!"

Cookie swung wide to the left, then whipped around the turn to the right onto the road. The dogs followed her well and I leaned the bike, popped my foot once, and made the corner like I'd been doing it all my life.

We went a mile on the gravel road, the speed holding, the old bike rattling and bouncing, and I started to gain confidence, became perhaps even a little cocky. The new dogs were running well. Ortho and Devil were absolutely churning up the road and Murphy surprisingly had that marvelous curve the tug makes up over the dogs when they are pulling well.

I began composing things I would tell Ruth when I returned. I would run them around the section road, four miles altogether, and she would be so surprised when I told her that the Canadian dogs—she hadn't believed in them ever since they ate the kennels— were working out. The bike was fun to ride, comfortable, I would tell her, the dogs were all wonderful, the sky was clear, I would probably win the Iditarod with such dogs . . .

A rabbit chose then, that instant, to run from one side of the road to the other; in all the world, of all the rabbits and all the roads, this rabbit chose that moment to cross this road in front of these dogs.

Cookie had seen rabbits a million times, knew what they were, and didn't fall for it. She went past the rabbit, although she did look at it, and even Max tried to follow her.

Not Ortho and Devil and Murphy. Devil hung a left and went after the rabbit, Ortho right with him and Murphy just half a beat behind.

Cookie tried to hold them but it was like trying to hold a train. She simply skidded backwards, took Max with her, and decided that if she wanted to live and keep her legs she'd better get out ahead of them and try to control them while they chased the rabbit.

It was the right decision but it still had disastrous effect. I was now in the position of going rabbit hunting sitting on a rusty 1957 Schwinn with a chrome tank and tattered handlebar tassels, being pulled through thick forest by five dogs.

There was never really any hope that I would make it. I tried. We hit a ditch and bounced, the whole bike in the air, and came down upright and somehow I managed to keep it upright.

Then the rabbit ran into thick willows and the dogs followed and I lost everything. In seconds I was on my side, then the bike was on top of me, bouncing, then I was back on top but not up on the wheels, just dragging, and then there was a pine limb about three feet off the ground that caught me somehow in the stomach and face at the same time and I was gone, face down, crumpled, while the bike and team disappeared with a great clatter through the forest.

It took me a moment to get my bearings and what remained of my wits about me. I heard the bike crashing for a time, fainter and fainter, then nothing, and decided I had to catch them and started walking.

Sooner or later, I figured, the bike would hang up on a tree or in the brush and I would catch up with them.

I was wrong. I hadn't reckoned on the power of the three Canadian dogs. I started following the trail — which was very easy to follow, helped by the sound of the bicycle dragging through the brush — and expected to see the bike and team any moment.

The trail crashed through willows, ran along a swamp for half a mile and then headed out *into* the swamp. I followed, soon waist deep in a grass and mud mixture called "loon shit" by the local people, wading where I knew the dogs must have been swimming, around snags and through more brush, mile after mile, the gouged, torn trail of the bicycle like a beacon before me.

Any moment, I kept saying, torn and eaten alive by mosquitoes, covered with wood ticks, ripped by thorns and brush — any moment I'd find them tangled and messed up and wouldn't they be glad to see *me* . . .

In four or five miles I came out to a highway and my heart sank when I saw the skid marks of the bicycle head out into traffic. Sled dogs have no concept of cars or traffic and I was sure they would be killed. But on the other side of the highway the marks moved across the shoulder and back into the woods and I followed gratefully.

Two more miles south they led, then kicked off along a power line heading straight east. It was now late evening and I was on foot, at least six rough woods miles from home, completely covered in mud and weeds and ticks and bug bites and still the trail led me on.

It kept moving east and I stayed with it until dark, and then after dark, followed by streaming hordes of mosquitoes so thick I couldn't breathe, until finally I simply couldn't see any longer and at last I admitted defeat.

I had lost my dog team.

They say you aren't a musher until your team has run off and left you, and while I had twice done that in the winter with the sled it was with the trapline team and they stopped after a bit and I could catch them. And once Cookie brought the team back around to me.

But this was different. These Canadian dogs most definitely marched to their own drum and it was clear they were never going to stop. All I could do now was go home and take a vehicle and start driving, try to find them the next day.

But home wasn't that accessible. I had walked three or four miles after crossing the highway and hitting the power line. It was now pitch dark and I was over ten miles from the house—the thought "lost" came to mind—in deep woods.

I thought briefly of making camp. But I had left the yard with no equipment, thinking only of a short run, and didn't have any matches or gear to camp. Without a fire and the small help of moving, the mosquitoes would drain me dry. As it was they had been at my eyes so much the eyelids were nearly swollen shut.

So I walked. In misery that I had lost what seemed to be remarkable pulling dogs, and Cookie, and even the lump-brain (as Ruth called him) Max, and I felt horrible.

And the walk did nothing to lift my spirits. The terrain was impossible. It took me three hours just to get back to the highway and then I compounded the error by deciding to take a shortcut through a pine forest rather than walk the ten or twelve remaining miles around on the roads.

The shortcut proved, as most of them seem to do, to be a "longcut" and put me in two more swamps of such depth and difficulty that at one point I had to swim in the mucky water for nearly two hundred yards.

I do not know how I found home. Indeed, I do not think I found it so much as mistakenly stumbled across it.

About three in the morning clouds came up and obscured what starlight had been available for seeing at least dim shadows. Somewhere around then I lost any touch with reality as far as location was concerned and went on full automatic. I'd walk until I bounced into something, turn, walk until I bounced, turn, walk until . . .

By pure chance one of the things I hit proved, just before dawn, to be our cabin.

I made my way inside, found a pot of coffee on the back of the stove and the stove still warm. I would have one cup, then take the car—we had an old Ford Maverick, given to us by a friend, that sometimes ran—and see if I could locate a farmer somewhere who had seen a dog team dragging a crumpled bike.

Ruth looked over the loft, half-asleep. "Oh, you're home. What time is it?"

The clock was over the windows. "Just short of six."

"In the morning?"

"Yes."

"Did you just get back?"

"Yes. I'm going to have some coffee and then go looking for the dogs . . ."

"What dogs?"

"The team. I lost them out there in the brush. They're probably halfway to New York by now."

"Oh no. They came back last night. I was just making some supper and I heard them drag the bike into the yard. Cookie took them right up to the kennel."

"She did?" I sat at the kitchen table, holding the coffee like a support beam.

"Yes. And Devil was so sweet. I unharnessed him and he licked my hand . . ."

A preliminary taste, I thought. Just checking for flavor.

". . . and wagged his tail when I hooked him to his chain. They're all fine. Did you have a rough night out there?"

My eyes were swollen shut, my lips twice their normal size, I had been raked by thorns and stickers, probably had worms from swallowing swamp water, and felt like I hadn't slept in over a month (a feeling I would learn to be a standard part of training for the Iditarod). Still, there was that other thing. The stupid thing. Pride.

"No. It was more or less normal."

The worst thing is that I would find my answer to be true.

Major Wrecks

We—the dogs and I—then entered a period that Ruth insists should be titled Major Wrecks. And in truth it would be a correct definition.

I was starting in ignorance, fueled by more ignorance and a major helping of incorrect information—one sprint musher who ran Irish setters told me dogs couldn't be fed meat, had to be fed only grain products to "keep their system clean"—and I compounded the error by trying to make wrong things right.

It started with building a rig. I talked to some sprint runners and used their ideas and came up with a nice, light, welded pipe thing that rode on wheelbarrow wheels; a tricycle arrangement with the front wheel steered by two pull-ropes.

A light rig is much easier to pull than a sled. On a hard road it rolls on ball bearings and the dogs barely feel it. Then I did as sprint runners did and ran large teams—ten, twelve, and fifteen dogs, adding on more as they came.

The difference in procedure is that sprint runners train only for short distances, at high speeds. They do not want to develop endurance muscles or toughness because it slows the dogs down and in sprint running speed is everything. I have actually seen teams of greyhounds wearing sweaters until it is time to run, screaming around a nine-mile track like bullets, only to be put back into their sweaters and warm beds when they are finished.

But because they never really develop their dogs from an endurance and strength standpoint, most sprint runners—the ones I asked for advice—really didn't understand just how strong, how tough sled dogs can be.

Napoleon once said good morale among troops is as four is to one, and something similiar happens to sled dogs. As they gain strength from training, and knowledge and confidence, as they understand that you will give them beef when they run and fat when they run and love when they run and your soul when they run, as they learn to feel that, understand that, *know* that, they become something completely different. They are no longer just sled dogs, or pets—they become distance dogs, dogs that cannot, will not be stopped.

When it first happens it is frightening—like watching Dr. Jekyll turn into Mr. Hyde. Their shoulders grow, they gain weight in both fat and, more important, muscle, and their coats sleek up with the added meat and fat (as much as they can eat when the training is going full bore). And they get *strong*—god, how strong.

The difference between a dog not trained for distance and one at full-distance stride is amazing—four, five, sometimes eight to one.

On a light rig, ten or twelve sprint dogs could be run easily. So I was told and so I did. But with distance dogs in good shape on the same rig you should never use over four or five—not if you expect to live. And the magic number—seven—should never be exceeded on anything less than a full car body (which I later used) with the engine gone. Something happens between the seventh and eighth dog that is truly phenomenal. A power curve is passed and with eight and up you're in a zone that defies control without special gear.

I knew none of this. Once I had the light rig I started getting dogs, adding them to the overall team as I found them.

Typhoon, Cookie, Yogi, Max, Storm, Steven, Bill, Devil, Murphy, Ortho, Big Mac, Raven, Byron—other people's dogs, other people's names. I didn't get to name a single dog from the team—although later we did have pups, many pups, and I got to pick names.

I ran them the way I thought I was supposed to run them, putting new sections of gangline on as each new dog or set of dogs arrived and just adding them to the team.

But a kind of infection of will had occurred that I

hadn't understood. I had the trapline team, the original seven. They had been nice dogs, happy dogs, peaceful dogs. I had worked them all winter and never had a problem with them, especially Cookie. I frequently brought her in the house and let her run loose. That original team was easy to control, though already very strong, and I thought it would help me to gain and maintain a control over the new dogs.

It went the other way. The trapline team became a distance team and the problem came about because they were already in shape from running all year. The other dogs, the new dogs, the wild dogs, the Canadian dogs, the native dogs swept the old trapline team up in their wonderful madness and I . . . I was just a part of the rig.

It was insane.

When I started to run eight dogs, then nine and ten—with the first three Canadian dogs—I realized something was different, something was hard to control. But when I added three more, running eleven on the light rig, and then two more after that, I entered a world that felt positively surreal.

"You look like a toy," Ruth said as I came back from being dragged out of the yard on my face, hanging on to the overturned rig. "A big doggie toy . . ." Out of the first twenty runs, I didn't once leave the yard in one piece.

My first run with a large team was the classic one, and should have warned me about the rest of them. I had decided to run them a little long. By this time it was cool enough during the days for extended running.

(I still did not understand running at night and indeed had been told by some that dogs were blind at night and couldn't see to run—totally erroneous.) So I thought I would try thirty miles. It isn't much—not even a third of the hundred or more miles first runs should be—but it seemed like a long way and I thought I should carry gear with me. I loaded the rig down with a backpack tied in place and a box of dog food, a tent, a rolled-up tarp, a winter coat—just in case it cooled off—pots and pans for cooking, a small ax, a bow saw, a lantern, a gallon of fuel for the lantern, and a full-size, two-burner Coleman stove.

I looked, and sounded, like a hardware store leaving the yard. But leaving the yard was as far as most of the stuff got.

I hooked up thirteen dogs. The rig was tied off to a tree with a stout rope and a quick release that I had checked at least four times.

The dogs were fired up and I hooked Cookie in first, let her hold the gangline out, then went for each dog and hooked them into position. Each new dog affected the other dogs until, by the time I'd harnessed ten of them, the din was deafening. More importantly, the sound, the urgency of the dogs was affecting me as well and by the time I had eleven and twelve in place and only one left—Devil—I was going back and forth from the kennel to the rig at a dead run, trying to hurry and let them run. Devil popped me as I reached for him, drew a little blood, but it was less than usual and I thought we might be getting on friendlier terms. I put him in the gangline, went to the rig, stood on it, waved to Ruth who was standing by the door of the house, and jerked the quick release loose.

I don't think the rig hit the ground more than twice all the way across the yard. My god, I thought, they've learned to fly. With me hanging out the back like a tattered flag we came to the end of the driveway, where we would have to turn, must turn onto the road.

The dogs made the turn fine.

The rig started to as well, but I had forgotten to lean into the turn and it rolled and once it rolled it kept rolling—it felt like two or three hundred times. I had time for one quick look back—it seemed like a dry goods store had blown up across the road and in the ditch—and grabbed at something to hold.

In some fashion I don't understand I hung on—I think because I'd lost them with the bike and was determined not to lose them again—and we set off down the road with the rig upside down, all the gear gone, and me dragging on the gravel on my face.

It took me four miles to get the rig up on its wheels, by which time the pipe-handlebar I had welded into position was broken off and I had nothing to hang on to but the steering ropes. I was also nearly completely denuded, my clothes having been torn to shreds during the dragging.

We did the thirty miles in just under two and a half hours and never once was I in anything like even partial control of the situation. Worse (or, as I was to find later, better), Cookie had started into heat. She didn't stop to breed—which she would do on subsequent runs—but it didn't matter. She ran ahead of

77

them and the males were excited by her and used every available opportunity to start what a musher would later tell me was called "a tits and balls-up war."

It was just a rolling dogfight, being led by this cute little wolfy bitch with her tail out to the side, with me hanging on the back with two ropes, half-naked, screaming obscenities, trying to get the fighting dogs to stop.

Later that fall, just before snow, Ruth and I sat talking about that first run with a big team on the light rig.

"It would have been nice," she said, sitting by the warm stove drinking coffee, "if that had been your worst run."

I nodded.

"Unfortunately it was your best."

"Well, not the best . . ."

"Yes, dear. It was."

In subsequent runs I left the yard on my face, my ass, my back, my belly. I dragged for a mile, two miles, three miles. I lost the team eight, ten times; walked twelve, seventeen, once forty-some miles looking for them. The rig broke every time we ran, torn to pieces, and I finally borrowed a welder and rebuilt the thing every night. Every farmer within forty miles of us knew about me, knew me as "that crazy bastard who can't hold his team." I once left the yard with wooden matches in my pocket and had them ignite as I was being dragged past the door of the house, giving me the semblance of a meteorite, screaming something about my balls being on fire at Ruth, who was laughing so hard she couldn't stand.

I thought it was me.

I had read some newspaper articles by this time and knew a little about Susan Butcher and others who ran the race, and I couldn't understand what difference there could be between their dogs and my dogs and why they seemed to be able to run theirs and I couldn't run mine.

I simply couldn't get out of the yard alive.

Finally, I saw a picture of a dog team training for the Iditarod in Canada in the early fall. There were fifteen dogs, all about the size of my dogs, hooked into a conventional gangline.

They were pulling a car.

A *whole* car. Motor, windshield, doors, the works. It even had a back seat. A couple was sitting in the car, leaning out the windows, out of the weather— most decidedly *not* dragging on their faces—and smiling at the camera.

A whole car.

I was by this time running fifteen dogs, seven of which were already strong, on a rig that weighed, at most, 120 pounds. The couple in the picture were pulling something that weighed over a ton with the same number of dogs. Perhaps more to the point, they were smiling and I had done little but grimace in terror for the last thirty or forty runs.

I took Ruth and left the house that night headed for town in the old Ford.

"Where are we going?" she asked.

"To a junkyard. We're going to pull a clunker home and make a rig. It's time to get serious about this training business."

We found an old English Ford at the junkyard. The engine was already gone, but there was air in all the tires and—most importantly—the brakes worked. The junkyard dealer donated it to the cause and we pulled it home and backed it up to the kennel. I took a few minutes to remove the doors to make entrance and exit faster.

In one of the articles I read that the dogs should be hooked to heavy loads with a spring or bungee line of some kind to take up the shock of starting. I didn't think a simple bungee system would work so I fashioned a hookup involving two complete truck-sized inner tubes—a bungee donut if you will—to take the load when they lunged.

I hooked the gangline to the front of this, locked the emergency brake and started hooking up dogs.

With Cookie on the front holding tight, when I came to the eighth dog I looked up to see the car starting to slide. I quickly found a rope and tied it to a tree and harnessed the rest of the dogs.

Ruth was watching and I waved her over. "Want to go for a ride?"

She looked at the car, at me, at the dogs and smiled. "I'll watch this time. Maybe when some of the bugs get worked out . . ."

"What bugs? It's a car—they'll pull it, we'll ride."

"I'll wait."

It would prove to be a wise decision.

I had learned something from my small-rig disasters and I chose not to carry any gear but just take them on a six-mile run on the gravel roads.

When all was ready I got in the car and pulled the quick release.

"Hike!" I yelled to the dogs, and they dutifully took off like they were on fire.

The car sat still.

For a moment.

I had forgotten to release the hand brake. I did this now, but in the meantime the dogs had stretched the two truck inner tubes until they looked like spaghetti.

"See?" I smiled at Ruth who was standing off to the side. *Well* off. "It's working like a charm . . ."

The inner tubes caught up and jerked the car ahead with a snatch that nearly tore my head off. This released the pull on the dogs and they shot ahead. The inner tubes stretched again. The car surged forward once more. The dogs slammed ahead. The inner tubes stretched. The car jerked . . .

I left the yard like a horizontal bungee jumper.

I had one image of Ruth bent over holding her stomach, laughing, near collapse, and then I was out of sight and sproinging down the road trying to think of a way to stop.

Left to my own devices I probably would never have solved the problem but it didn't matter. We made the loop in an hour and a half and by the time we got back the dogs had figured it out and would start slowly until the tubes caught up and the car was moving, gradually increasing speed.

When we returned I worked a rope into the bungee system to make a limit to the stretching. Ruth came out while I was working.

"I'm going to run long tonight and camp with them. I'll head back tomorrow. Probably be in around ten in the morning."

She nodded and started to say something but hesitated.

"What?"

"Nothing."

"No, really. What were you going to say?"

"You sound so definite. Don't you think it would be better if you didn't plan things? Just say you're going to run them and not how long or how far? Every time you've done this and planned on something the dogs take over and it comes out some other way . . ."

"It's different this time. I've got the car, control. Don't worry."

And in truth I actually believed it.

We left the yard just at dark. I had read about running at night and rigged up a battery with a hand-held spot so I could watch them run and make sure everything was working out all right.

And, surprise of surprises, it was working exactly as planned. I had hooked up all fifteen of them and within a couple of miles they were settled in and working and I was leaning back in the comfort of the seat thinking that it would be nice if I had brought something to read. If the run kept going like this I could probably sleep. They were holding about six miles an hour pulling the heavy car and I thought I would let them run for three hours and then take a break and feed and water them, let them sleep a bit, maybe hook them up again at midnight or so . . .

God, it was great. For the first time I could actually think in terms of a big team, an Iditarod-class team, without terror in my soul. I was running on secondary and logging roads, back into the woods and there was no traffic to contend with, absolutely nothing that could go wrong that I couldn't handle.

I think this was similiar to the thinking I did when I enlisted in the army—only a little drunk—and got to spend three years, eight months, twenty-one days, and nine hours regretting it.

The fall is a time of intense activity in the woods. Deer fight and breed, bears romp around eating anything and everything they can get before hibernating, moose look for something to kill (more on this later), and skunks travel looking for winter fat and a place to sleep.

They are everywhere, skunks, and because of their ability to stink they have been largely ignored by naturalists and popular writers. Everybody says they're cute, stink like hell, seem to carry rabies a lot, and that's about it. There is much more about them than is publicly known. Everything eats them—canines, for instance, coyotes, fox, wolves all seem to have a taste for fresh skunk, the stinkier the better. But there is one fact that becomes even more important where running sled dogs is concerned.

Skunks are nocturnal.

I had never spent much time in the woods awake and moving at night. When I camped I stopped, made a fire, slept. Dogs changed all that. Suddenly I found myself out there, moving, covering vast amounts of territory in the dark with fifteen furry friends out ahead of me.

So the principal parts of the pattern for disaster are there: a complacent (some might say stupid) man galloping around in the woods in the dark, a fired-up canine team eager to see what's over the next rise, and apparently every skunk in the western hemisphere moving along in the blackness on the same track as the team.

We hit the first skunk about nine o'clock.

I was just reaching down to adjust the seat back a little—the Ford had recliners and I was thinking of getting more comfortable, wondering if it would be possible to actually doze while they were running (a bit of idiocy so total as to defy belief)—when I got the first sulfurous whiff.

It was so sudden, such a surprise, that I didn't for some reason associate it with a skunk at first and by the time I recognized it for what it was, it was too late.

The front end of the team, Cookie and the point dogs, went crazy. I flipped the light on and aimed it up a bit but there was such confusion and noise that I couldn't understand anything.

I locked the emergency brake—almost needless since the team had stopped pulling and were fighting over the skunk—and ran to the front of the team.

Cookie was winning. She had the skunk by the shoulders and was trying to hold it but at the same time I arrived Devil caught up. He was hooked back in the team and he virtually pulled the whole rig forward, brakes locked and all, and grabbed the skunk away from Cookie.

Without thinking I jerked at the skunk to pull it away from Devil. This was risky in itself. Devil considered the skunk to be food, was in fact trying to swallow the skunk whole, or so it seemed, and grabbing Devil's food amounted to suicide.

But worse, I grabbed the tail, which had the effect of swinging the rear end of the skunk around to aim the potent business end at me, at my face.

Whereupon the skunk let go.

His firepower was somewhat diminished, as he'd dumped some of it on the dogs, but there was still a hefty load and it blew, like the winds of death, directly into my face.

"Gaaacck!"

It was exactly that sound. I have never heard it duplicated by another person, and it was accompanied by projectile vomiting, walking in circles in the ditch, trying to rub it out of my eyes, and a sudden and sincere wish to become an investment banker, or any other job that would never put me close to a skunk's ass again.

It took a half-hour to get some vision and ability to breathe right, and another half-hour to sort the team and untangle them and get them ready to continue on.

It was bad, it was vile, it was in some way green and bilious, but we had overcome it and, I thought, could now finish the run—stinking, perhaps, still queasy and sick, but none the worse for wear in other ways.

We hit the second skunk within a mile.

The results were almost exactly the same except that this time the skunk somehow got away from the dogs on his own and I tried to help it by kicking it down into the ditch, out of the way, so it could escape.

Rule one: don't grab a skunk by the tail and pull.

Rule two: don't kick a skunk.

It sprayed me full up the front, a goodly load again hitting my face, and I immediately started vomiting once more, rubbing my eyes, trying to find the dogs and rigs.

Another half-hour to get my systems cleared, another half-hour to untangle the dogs, compounded by Devil biting me because he'd missed a chance at the second skunk and blamed me.

Another mile or so down the road.

Another skunk.

All in all we hit six skunks that first night and at least five of them got me. I was drenched in stink, soaked in it, and by four in the morning I'd had enough. We hadn't run more than eight miles and I turned on a road through the woods that headed home.

By this time the dogs considered the whole venture a chance to hunt skunks and we smoked down the roads, waiting for the next one, and hit the yard doing twenty or so.

I unharnessed them and put them away and went to the cabin. Ruth was still in bed in the loft and I didn't want to awaken her but the instant I walked in the door I heard:

"What in the name of god is that smell?"

"It's just me."

She peered over the loft. "What happened to you?"

I looked back up at her, reeking, standing in the

fumes that somehow made me see things in a yellow cast, my eyes swollen from being sprayed.

"Skunks," I said. "Skunks happened to me. A lot of skunks."

"Are the dogs all right?"

"The dogs . . ." I started to turn but the movement made more odor come out of my clothing and I stopped ". . . are all right. We won't have to feed Devil for a month."

"Why?"

"He ate the skunks."

"*Ate* them?"

"Yes."

"Couldn't you stop him?"

"Not without artillery."

I finally decided to hell with the odor, the clothes had to come off. I started undressing.

"What are you doing?"

"Coming to bed."

"*Here?*"

I stopped. "Where else?"

She let her breath out and I realized she had been holding it all this time. "Couldn't you kind of, you know, for a night or two, sleep outside?"

"With the dogs?"

She smiled. "I knew you'd understand."

"In the kennel?"

She nodded, pulling back under the covers. "You're so smart about these things."

I stood for another minute, then turned and went back outside, stopping at the English Ford to pick up my sleeping bag and thermos before heading for the kennel, stomping along in a cloud of odor and self-pity, not realizing that what had happened would prove to be the best possible twist of all possible fates concerning the dogs and the Iditarod.

Becoming Dog

I had camped with the dogs many times, and they had come to understand it as a way of life. First they were tied to trees, then I lit a fire, fed them, then uncurled the bag in the sled or on foam pads or in the fall on a pile of leaves, and we all slept until morning, and it was daylight when we would go back to work.

This was radically different.

This was the kennel. I had never slept here before. When they were in kennel—where each dog was on a chain and had its own house—I always went to the house and they went to their houses and we all slept until the next time we would see each other.

This time I didn't go away and it altered the way they saw me, felt about me, thought of me and my actions, and changed the way I thought as well—started me thinking right.

Started me thinking in terms of dog and not human.

It was a clear night; stars splattered across the sky in the brightness that can only come from the cold taking the humidity out of the air. Brilliant spots of light that seemed just over head high.

I considered where to sleep. The dogs whimpered a bit and when it became clear that I wasn't going to feed or pet them they settled and sat and watched me. They were, to the last dog, putrid. Luckily it didn't get to me because I reeked as well—I honestly didn't think I would ever be able to smell anything other than skunk again—and I moved through them looking for a place to put the bag down.

I settled next to Devil. There was no particular reason for it, other than the fact that the ground was level there, flat, and it seemed like a decent place to sleep. I put the foam pad down and the bag on top of it and shucked my coveralls and shoepacs and slid in. Next to me I arranged footgear and I poured a cup of tea from the thermos and propped up on one elbow to sip tea and look at the sky and the kennel, life, everything.

Devil was sitting directly in front of me, staring at me.

"Hi." It was just serendipity, a silliness, but he jumped like I'd screamed at him.

And his tail wagged.

It was the first time I'd seen his tail wag since he'd come to us and I smiled.

"How are you?"

Another wag. What the hell, I thought, he's being friendly. I reached out to pet him. The tail stopped wagging instantly and he growled, soft thunder, and I pulled my hand back. Another dog—I couldn't tell who—answered the growl and then a third and somebody (I thought Cookie) started a small song, just a night song, and they all joined in. I leaned my head back and joined, harmonizing the best I could— though still not as well as most of them could do it— and they didn't stop but kept singing and I kept singing with them for three or four minutes.

Whereupon they all stopped, suddenly, and caught me with a note hanging. I felt foolish and looked at Devil, who was still sitting there, watching me.

"I didn't know you were going to stop."

He wagged his tail, cocked his head, and looked at my face.

"I don't know things yet." An understatement that. "You guys will have to teach me . . ."

And I realized when I said it that I meant it. What I needed to learn only the dogs could teach me, and I'm not sure if it was then or later in the night when I awakened once to see them all still sitting, staring at me, that I decided what I had to do.

I had to sleep in the kennel. I had to be with the dogs all the time, learn from them all the time, know them all the time. More than sleep, I had to *live* in the kennel.

I had to in some way become a dog.

And in some strange way it had to come from Devil; he was the key. If I could understand him, get him to know and accept me, I would be on the way, or at least started.

That day I dozed some and worked on the rig and gear and that night we ran again. Not long—or as Ruth put it, just a "two-skunker" run—and when we came back to the kennel and I put the dogs away and went for my gear I carried it all to Devil's circle and moved in.

He immediately growled and climbed on top of his house. Ruth came out with a cup of tea and watched me, shaking her head.

"You're going to sleep with Devil?"

I placed my foam pad on the ground and the sleeping bag on top of it. Devil growled again.

"By morning we're going to be old friends," I said—understating a bit. Actually, by morning he had pulled the foam pad out from beneath me and shredded it and opened the whole bottom end of my down bag and spread feathers over his entire circle. But I didn't know that then.

Ruth stared at me for a moment, then shook her head and went back into the house and I lay back to sleep, Devil sitting on his house like a gargoyle, visions of Iditarods dancing through my head.

❊ ❊ ❊

Living with the dogs proved to be easier than I thought it would be.

At first there was some adjusting. I had, for instance, to sew up my bag and get a new foam pad after the night with Devil. And establishing territory was difficult. Farley Mowat talked of trying to outpiss wolves in his book *Never Cry Wolf*—how he needed to establish a boundary and they kept marking over his urine. There is much of the wolf in sled dogs, especially the dogs down from Canada with the yellow eyes, and I noticed once that after I had pissed near the kennel every dog tried to get over to cover it. They'd drag me over to the side even when I was trying to run them down to harness them and piss on top of where I'd gone. This was carried to new heights by Cookie. She covered me, I covered her, she covered me, I covered her, and on and on until I was out and couldn't piss more, whereupon she covered me once more, scratched back with her feet and walked away, done and done. We fought the piss wars, cover on cover, for three or four days—until, as with Mr. Mowat, I had drunk enough tea to flush a radiator.

I thought that they should see me do all things, to know me, and the same for me watching them. I made a little table on fence posts in the middle of the kennel and put a hibachi with a small wok on top and cooked all my meals there, rain or shine, night or day.

First I'd feed the dogs, then I'd fire up the hibachi and cook on the wok and talk to the dogs while I worked.

"A touch of garlic, Wilson—makes everything good."

And Wilson—a big white dog with a dark eye patch—would stare at me as if I'd gone mad. (An interesting aside: I found that a touch of garlic *did* help dogs to eat when they didn't feel like eating; a bottle of powdered garlic became one of those dog things I carried with me all the time.)

I read in the kennel, sewed in the kennel, slept, and even set up a bathroom and did that in the kennel.

One day, between runs, I was working in the kennel and it started to rain and I ran for the house. I hadn't gone twenty yards when they set up a mournful howling and when I turned back they stopped. It became evident that they wanted me to stay, and I went back to the kennel and got wet. After that I did as the dogs did—just took what came.

It sounds simple but it proved to be another major breakthrough. Weather, trail, life—it all seemed the same. If I tried to change it, get away from it, I would lessen my effectiveness; by accepting, rolling with it, and making the best of it, things always seemed to work out for the better.

From that point on—rain or no rain, snow or no snow, storms, sleet, comfort or wounds or hardship—nothing stopped us.

We ran.

And in the running, in the push of it, we learned.

First Snow

$\int$now came early that fall—came early with cold weather and stayed and never hardened. In northern Minnesota it doesn't seem to snow much at a time; three or four inches. But it doesn't melt. And it snows every fourth or fifth day so within two weeks a buildup occurs that can be the start of truly deep snow. There have been times in the northern woods that by spring the snow stood eighty or ninety inches deep, all at three or four inches at a time, all so soft and fluffy that if you step off your snowshoes you go in well over your head and have a hell of a time getting back up.

This year looked to be starting that way. A night came in the fall when it dropped well below normal temperatures for the season, hung at about ten or fifteen below. Usually with that temperature in the fall it didn't snow. But the same night as the drop it started to snow, large, soft flakes that never seemed to settle but stayed light and airy.

In the morning there were four or five inches—too deep for a wheeled rig to run, but still too new and fluffy for a sled. There would be no control, no braking, no hold-back to slow the dogs.

"Wait until tomorrow," Ruth said. "Another day won't hurt."

But it was first snow. First sled snow. First time in the year to get on sleds and the urge was too strong. The dogs love the cold, run best at twenty, thirty below, and they were singing the new-snow songs trying to get me out of the house and into the kennel to run.

The pull was too strong. In the end I couldn't stand it and I suited up and took the harnesses from the ceiling racks where we hung them to dry and walked out into the bright morning.

The dogs went wild when they saw me carrying the harnesses, absolutely insane, and their enthusiasm— screaming, tearing around in their circles on the ends of their chains—quickly infected me and while walking from the house to the kennel I made a decision, or a series of decisions, that would nearly cost me my life and any chance to run the Iditarod.

I would go ahead and team them up.

This concept, forming the Iditarod team and running them as a whole unit, is one that is always in the back of the mind—you know you have to do it sooner or later. You must do it before the race, obviously—

you must use a larger team in the race to have any chance of finishing.

But the first time on a sled should be controlled, and there should be help. It's one thing to run them on a car body that weighs close to a ton. It's very much another to stick the same team on a sled that weighs less than ten percent of the car—and absolutely mad to do this with first snow, new snow, where there is no brake control, no steering ability.

What I should have done was six or seven dogs, on a heavy sled, loaded with gear—similiar to the trapline team; run two, three teams, alternate them and run them for two or three days until they were settled in and there was perhaps more snow or it had frozen so the brakes and hook would work. A sensible approach.

Instead, caught up with the dogs' screaming, I decided to team them up and run the same team as I would try to run in the race. Out of my yard, fresh out of the kennel, all the dogs absolutely packed with piss and vinegar and tearing to run.

I have no excuse for this idiocy except that something about the cold and the snow and the sun and the dogs made me think in such a way.

I did one thing that in the end saved me. I did not use a light sled. We had over the year become sponsored by many individuals and groups; when word of our attempt became known in the nearby town of Bemidji, Minnesota, it seemed that hundreds of wonderful people wanted to help us. There were gifts of tires, gear for dogs, dogs themselves, dog food, human food, tons and tons of meat and fat for the team, and what would sadly become perhaps the most important ingredient other than dogs—money. There were dances and picnics and potlucks to help out. People would stop me on the street and hand me ten dollars.

"For the race."

Always that. "For the race. Go up and run it— here, for the race."

Ten, five—sometimes one or two dollars. Jars were placed in businesses around town with labels that read:

HELP RUN THE IDITAROD

Quarters, nickels—all of it went for the dogs, for the race.

And sleds.

I made one sled, using boiled and steamed birch, and somebody gave me another one—a light racing sled. The racing sled weighed twelve pounds—a sprint sled with long tails (the runners stuck out well in back of the foot) which made it hard to steer. The sled I had made was more on the order of a toboggan with runners, copied from pictures I had seen of Susan Butcher's sleds (might as well copy the best), and weighed close to twenty-five pounds. Both sleds had Teflon-like plastic runner shoes that made them slick enough to almost slide on level ground and small claw brakes that would do little but hold the sled back off the wheel dogs on a downhill slope.

Had I taken either of the two sleds for this initial teamed-up run—considering the weather, the snow conditions, and the enthusiasm of the dogs—I probably would have been killed or at least seriously injured.

Instead, I dragged the heavy oak work sledge I had used for trapping to a tree by the kennel. I tied it off with a stout rope and a slipknot quick-release and spread the long gangline I had used for pulling the car in front of the sledge. Ruth—shaking her head all the time—helped me harness. I began hooking the dogs into their tugs, lead first—Cookie—then on back, hooking each dog in carefully.

The dogs acted strangely. They still lunged and wanted to go but they also waited and watched, watched as I would go to the kennel and get the next dog, bring it down, hook it in position, watched until I was down to the last two dogs. Then they went mad, totally bonkers. (I would see them get this crazy only once more—in the starting chutes in Anchorage.)

Ruth stopped. She had been going for the last dog and she stopped and turned to look at the team, her eyes wide with alarm.

They had changed.

They were perhaps not what they would be, would have to be for the race, but they were by god not what they used to be either.

They were a team.

And they knew it, felt it, screamed it. One sweet female named Tashia, always quiet and soft, was baring her teeth, taking great mouthfuls of snow and shaking her head, growling and tearing, trying to jerk the sled loose, rip the snow loose, tear the world loose and run. *Run.*

Some dogs were so frustrated they turned and grabbed the gangline, tugging at it to loosen the sled.

In a trance now, almost shock, some fear, I went to the sled. Ruth was by the front end, holding the dogs out so they wouldn't tangle. I looked at her and nodded, motioned for her to move away to the side.

Ruth stared across the din at me, silently mouthed the phrase, the question, *Are you sure?*

And truth be told I wasn't. I was, as a matter of fact, never so unsure in my life.

But now, I thought—*but now . . .*

. . . or never.

And I nodded, grabbed the sled with my left hand, stood to the runners, and jerked the quick-release slipknot.

Jesus.

Never anything like that. Never with horses, nor planes, nor hotted Harleys—never with anything in the world was it like that.

They didn't feel me back there. Sled, gear, my weight—we simply didn't exist for them.

They were gone.

They hit the end of the driveway wide open, hung a left, or started to. Cookie pulled them out trying to get down the road and then recognized our old trapline sled trail from the year before (we had not run it yet because there had been no snow) and with great joy left the road and ripped into the woods followed by fourteen wild dogs and one screaming man on a sled.

I didn't make ten feet before I hit the first tree, a foot-thick oak that didn't give at all. The sled, made of glue and bolted oak, likewise did not give.

I gave.

I had seen a U.S. Forestry survey of the tree count in the north woods—tens of thousands per square mile—and I hit every single one of them. Or so it seemed.

There never was even a semblance of control or steering. I simply tried to hang on and stay alive. And even that was a failure.

Cookie—gloriously free, running wild now, coursing with the ancient blood of wolves in her veins—ran in front of a pack of fourteen, ran where she wanted to run, as fast as she wanted to run.

She ran the trapline I had worked the winter before when I still trapped; the line she knew from memory. On a topographic map I had scaled the line and without figuring in hills or side trips it was just under seventy miles. Running the line, stopping to do sets, rest the dogs, load and unload gear—a normal run— usually took four days. On the best run, hurrying to get back for visiting company, we had done it in three days, sixteen hours.

This time we ran the whole line, side trips, hills and all, in six and a half hours.

Much, most of it I did not see—and those parts I did see were mostly blurred.

I was terrified. Not just of being injured—although that was a primary ingredient—but for the dogs. There was so much power, so much speed, and so little control that I worried a dog might swing out and catch a tree, be hurt. (Indeed, I would see a dog on another team killed this way during the race.)

Two moments stand out.

Down a long hill, standing on the brake, holding the sledge back off the dogs, and Devil went down, tripped and fell in a snow plume.

Oh, god, I thought. *Oh, god, he's down and the sled will take him, crush him.* And then, in that part of a minute, part of a second, Murphy, who ran next to Devil, Murphy who never seemed aware of anything, Murphy reached across the gangline, grabbed Devil's harness by the X on his back, and snatched him to his feet; an instant reaction, one that almost certainly saved Devil's life, and one that I had never seen before and never saw again.

Then later, a moment of confidence; we had come thirty, forty miles, still at a lope, still driving hard. I had no real control as yet, but I knew where we were now and what Cookie intended to do. I had arranged both feet on the runners, kept them on somehow, had both hands locked on the handlebar of the sled, had in some miraculous fashion managed to actually *miss* a tree or two and I straightened up to look at the team.

A mistake.

The moment I looked up, the tails of the sled runners dropped off in a one-foot ditch. Both of my feet moved into the air for a split second, the runners kicked sideways, and my feet came down on the snow and stopped dead.

I was still holding on to the handlebar and as my feet shot to the rear I came down on my hands. They were in turn jarred loose by the jolt and for an instant I was separated from the sled. I flailed with my hands and in panic I dislodged the snowhook from its leather pouch on the handlebar. It was tied directly into the

Stopping for gas at the highest point along the Alcan on our way to the race.

Camping out with the team during training, about a week before the race.

The team, two days before the race.

Top row, from left: Ready to start the race in downtown Anchorage.
The first night of the race, just before dark. Repairing harnesses after a fight.

Bottom row, from left: Food bags await us at the Finger Lake checkpoint.
Running the first hundred miles of the race, headed for the Alaska Range.

Top row, from left: Near the summit at Rainy Pass. Approaching Dalzell Gorge. Wilson, in front, after crossing the Alaska Range.

Bottom row, from left: The Burn: ninety-two miles of bad terrain. Beginning the 300-mile run across the Alaskan interior.

Top row, from left: The Shageluk council hall, where I nearly overdosed on moose chili. Battling wind on the Yukon River, where temperatures at night drop to 65 below. A food cache in the coastal village of Unalakleet.

Bottom row, from left: Running on sea ice on Norton Sound. Heading north on tundra toward the Bering Sea.

Wilson catches some rest, along with another musher and his team.

Dusk in the interior.

gangline on a ten-foot, thousand-pound test rope, and the hook described a perfect arc and fell off to the right side of the sled and landed with one of the points directly on top of my foot.

Snowhooks are designed to be self-setting so the harder the dogs pull the deeper they set. To compound the problem a friend had told me that if the points were needle-sharp the hook would set in lake ice; I had filed the points to be like tapered needles.

And one of these sharpened points now landed on top of my rubber shoepac. It went in like it had hit butter, pierced the rubber boot, then the felt lining and "set" itself. Falling back I watched in horror and waited for the pain.

It did not come.

Somehow the felt lining and heavy wool sock deflected the point, slid it forward where it passed neatly between my big and second toe, then punched through the bottom of the boot.

I went back and down off the sled, bounced once so hard it blew the air out of my lungs, felt a horrendous jerk on my right leg, and began dragging in back of the sled (or, as Ruth put it later, started trolling for wolves).

I tried pulling myself up, grabbed at the rope, the hook, anything, but it was no use. The snow and the speed of the dogs dragged me back and no matter how I fought I couldn't get up. Within moments my clothes were packed with snow—it came in my trouser legs, down my sleeves, around my neck. I must have looked like the Pillsbury doughboy, round and packed, but it probably saved my life.

The dogs didn't slow. Indeed, they seemed to increase speed—seemed to take a perverse delight in my predicament. On corners they would swing wide and "crack the whip" as they went around.

I, of course, was the tip of the whip and on many corners I established intimate relationships with trees. Whipping around added to my speed and I was slammed into the trees with something approaching terminal velocity. The only reason I wasn't hurt more—I bruised three ribs and had some cuts and abrasions on my face—was the shock-absorbing nature of the snow packed inside my clothing.

I do not know how long I dragged. Twice I hit my head hard enough to lose at least partial consciousness.

It was minutes—five, ten—but it seemed to be hours. I had no control, no hope, and had just fallen back, trying to hold my legs together, my head wrapped in my arms for protection. All I could do was hang there and wait, bouncing back and forth on the end of the rope.

A deer saved me. A deer and luck.

A doe jumped out of some red willows on the side of the trail and bounded across. Normally Cookie would not have turned, would have let it go. But she wasn't acting anything like normal, and the deer was so close—nearly jumping over Cookie.

She couldn't stand it. Without breaking stride she threw herself after the deer. She lunged off the trail, jerking the two point dogs after her. They in turn went for the deer and in half a second the whole team was off the trail charging through the willows.

They did not stop. But the doe took two spring-leaps and was gone over the willows. There was no trail. The willows were set as thick as hair and Cookie, realizing there was no way through, immediately zigged back out to the trail, the team following in a spray of snow and crashing willows.

The sled stopped, hesitated while the dogs were in and working out of the willows, and I grabbed the hook rope, pulled myself up, clawed up still farther, and caught the handlebar and jerked up and onto the runners and we were off again, careening through the forest.

I hooked my left arm through the handlebar, pushed my left foot down on the runner to wedge myself in, and worked the hook out of my boot while we moved. The rest of the trip I spent alternately hanging on for my life and shaking packed snow out of my clothing.

✳   ✳   ✳

Later that night I sat by the wood cookstove in the kitchen and sipped hot chocolate. We had come into the kennel as we had gone out—at a full run. Ruth had helped unharness them and I had fed them and we talked now; or I did while Ruth listened, nodding quietly from time to time.

"They never get tired," I said. The stove was wonderfully warm on my face and I was fighting sleep. "Never, they just don't wear down. Seventy miles at a dead run. I think I could have turned them around and run it backwards. I don't know . . ."

"Don't know what?"

"Anything. If I can hold them, run them. I don't know *them* any longer. They've become something wild. Even Cookie—she's changed, altered, entered some kind of a second state or something. I simply don't know her."

Ruth sighed. "Maybe that's the way it's supposed to be. Maybe for the race they have to be that way."

"It's . . ." I started to say more, say that it was frightening but there was something else to it as well. Something more than fear.

"It's what?" she prompted.

"I don't know exactly. Something more . . . it's exciting. Almost takes my breath away."

Ruth smiled. "You know what I think your biggest problem will be?"

"What?"

"Stopping them when you get to Nome."

I laughed because it seemed so preposterous. We were still sitting in Minnesota. Virtually broke. No real way to even get to Alaska let alone run the race. It was easy to joke about it—like whistling through a graveyard. So far it was still all talk—very far from happening. We had looked many times at Nome on the map, read articles in *Alaska* magazine about the race. It all seemed alien. Like the moon—a whole other world.

"Yeah," I said. "Nome . . ."

Alaska

Sleep died early. Before the race, before the starting chutes, before Anchorage, and before even Alaska, sleep died.

Training in Minnesota killed it some. Long nights that fed into longer days and still longer nights until they were all mixed and made normal sleep almost impossible. But the desire was still there. One unforgettable morning, standing to the sled just after dawn, it became impossible to discern if it was truly morning or afternoon—it had all blended in exhaustion, and confusion dominated until only a look at the compass showed the sun was in the east and proved it was morning. The wish for sleep to come was still in the mind, the dream of sleep was alive.

The drive to Alaska killed it.

An old truck was donated—a 1960 Chevy half ton with salt rot so bad the floor was gone and the seats were sitting on the ground. A friend was a mechanic and he rebuilt the truck; old stainless steel cafeteria trays were bolted in for a floor and a welder helped by fixing up an old dog trailer, also donated—so much was given, donated, handed over that it became difficult to remember who gave what (and for those who gave who read this: thank you, for everything).

It still did not seem to be happening, did not seem possible that it could happen.

Even, at last, in the yard. The truck was loaded, packed, already experiencing what is known as "rookie bulge"—loaded so full that the rear end was bottomed out and rested directly on the axle. Extra food, extra sleeping bags, extra *everything*. The trailer was hooked up to the truck, the dogs—twenty of them now, all tough, all ready—were loaded, the truck was running; the man who donated the truck was coming with me to Alaska, as was a boy who had decided to help and handle the dogs.

Ruth came to the driver's side of the truck. "Drive carefully." There was real concern in her eyes—as there should have been. We were sitting in a truck with a six-cylinder engine, a three-speed transmission, plain tires with a set of discount store chains, and we were going to leave northern Minnesota and drive up through Canada, through the Yukon, up the Alcan Highway in the dead of the worst part of winter—it would be sixty below in the Yukon when we got there; so cold the truck heater did nothing and we had to constantly scrape the ice off the *inside* of the windshield while we drove just to see where we were going.

It took eight days. And nights. Driving around the clock, stopping to lie beneath the truck on the ice of the Alcan—they do not plow it down to the surface but leave a layer of packed snow-ice to drive upon—to fight the chains, tugging them into position, driving in low gear at two miles an hour to the top of an ice mountain, then stopping to remove the chains for the long run down, then stopping to put the chains on again and into low gear . . .

Endlessly. Taking the dogs out of the trailer every four or five hours to let them shake out and pee. Then back in, grinding on the road.

Twice it seemed we could not make it. A piece of metal stuck down in the overloaded trailer and in some manner on a certain kind of bump rammed into the tire and blew it. We ate tires, slept tires, went through six tires on the trailer before we figured out what was happening.

The drive proved disastrously expensive, tore into, raped the money we had saved for the race. Before getting to Alaska, in the town of Fort Nelson, British Columbia, it was evident I was going to be broke when we got there and that we would not be able to run the race.

I sat with the man who gave us the truck. He had a wife, two daughters, was a concrete worker and worked harder than anybody I knew for every dime he made.

"Uhhh," he coughed. Often he was quiet—sometimes passed a morning without saying a word. "Seems a shame to come this far and not go all the way."

"We're shredding money . . ."

"My wife and I have some savings."

"God, man, you can't . . ."

"Yes." He stands. The decision was made. "We can. I'll call her and ask her but I know she'll agree."

And so we ground on until at last, somehow, we came to the border checkpoint going into Alaska, and the guard came out smiling at our truck, our trailer, us—we had to be fully suited up, parkas, mukluks, hoods up, masks, and all, just to ride *inside* the truck.

"Nice rig," he said. And of course he was being sarcastic. We had used cans of flat black spray paint to color the truck, fabricated a homemade plywood shell for the rear—it was easily the ugliest vehicle I had ever seen. But not then. Not at that moment. I looked at it and thought of what it had done—we were now only five or six hundred miles from where the race started—and I nodded at the guard and with not a little pride in my voice I said, "Yeah—thanks."

And finally, completely fried from lack of sleep, never to sleep right again, worn beyond sleep, thinking only tire chains and tires and more tires and dogs in and out of the trailer endlessly fed and watered, finally, *finally* we were in Alaska.

Where it all began.

❉   ❉   ❉

People, all people in Alaska, people having to do with the race, people in stores, people met on streets were all, everyone I met, wonderfully hospitable and enormously helpful. Had they not been this way I would never in my apalling ignorance have made the starting chutes, let alone the race.

It started with them not laughing at us. I cannot look back on it now without laughing, and I am amazed that they could have kept straight faces. We arrived in Wasilla, Alaska, where the race headquarters was located, with a truck literally falling apart. When we released the bungee cords holding it together the doors fell off, and yet when we went inside to sign up and tell them we had arrived one of the volunteers looked up and merely said, "Oh, yes. We heard you were coming. They say you have a bad truck but good dogs."

One thing became strikingly clear. I knew nothing, less than nothing, about running dogs long distances. Indeed, much of what I had learned in training was wrong.

First, and foremost, the race is truly about nurturing, caring for the dogs. They are everything, all of everything, and it wasn't enough to merely schlep them some food and let them rest—which was pretty much what I had been doing. Every aspect of every dog needs to be considered. Feet, teeth, conditioning, toenails, coat, wounds (from fighting—a constant problem—or trail injury). Nor is this a one-time appraisal. Feet must be examined on the half-hour while they are running, tipped up so they are in the light from the headlamp, the toes spread to look up inside them, into the web of the foot for signs of irritation, close examination beneath the nail, along the sides of the pads, up beneath the hairline on the foot. Every toe. On every foot. On every dog. Every thirty minutes. Ankles and shoulders rubbed—hands on dogs, touching dogs, feeling dogs, all the time, anytime the team is stopped, hands and eyes to dogs.

There is an old saying about sailors working in the rigging of tall sailing ships. It was so frightening up high that some of them simply clung to the rigging and the mate would cry from below: "One hand for you, one hand for the ship!"

I quickly found that with dogs, with running them, it is *no* hands for the musher and all hands, eyes, mind, soul—everything for the dogs.

After signing in and getting some of the tons of paperwork and handouts and instructions from the headquarters—much of which was almost pure Greek to me—we traveled north and camped in an area where there were many other Iditarod mushers training.

It was late December. The race did not start until the first Saturday in March, and had it not been for those two months in the bush, running dogs and seeking assistance, it would have been impossible. I begged help. A musher would come by to say hi and stop to rest his dogs and I would pump him—or her, there were several women training in the same area—for information. Anything. Everything. Tidbits. How to use booties correctly. How to feed correctly. Water them. And the one question most difficult to answer:

What was the race like?

Really like?

And always they would look at me—men, women, old and young, any who had finished it or started it and been unable to finish it (and there were many of these)—always they would look and their eyes would get what is called in the military "the thousand-yard stare" and sometimes they would smile and sometimes there would be a shot of something else (fear, perhaps, or amazement) and they would open their mouths and say:

"Well . . ."

And stop. It was not that they didn't want to help—everybody helped us, bent over backward (especially when they saw how incredibly ignorant I really was). But the race is . . . different. I did not understand it then (and indeed, am only beginning to understand it now) but it is truly different. From everything. And still now, if asked what it is like I nod and smile and get that tinge of fear/amazement in my eyes and open my mouth and say:

"Well . . ."

And stop. It is almost impossible to articulate the race as a whole. It can be broken down into sections, days, hours, horrors, joys, checkpoints, winds, nights, colds, waters, ices, deaths, tragedies, small and large courages. But as a whole, to say generally what the race is like, there are no exact words.

Outrageous, perhaps. Staggering. Insane. Altering.

All of them, and more. No one word works. But given time, given the time to stare out across nothing and think, they would start.

"It was at Rohn River. I found god there. Coming down off Rainy Pass onto Rohn River the temperature dropped from forty above to sixty-five below and I came around a corner and it hit me and my feet froze—that's where I lost my little toes—and both runners on my sled broke and I was dragged for two miles in back of the broken sled and . . ." Pause to breathe. The stare came back. "So watch it on Rohn River."

And it came then. What was described, the whole event, losing toes and being dragged and getting close to god, the whole thing took perhaps twenty minutes. In a run of eighteen or so days, of Christ knows how many twenty-minute segments, this one bit of advice that cost toes to learn took only twenty minutes to happen. *Is it all this way? Is it all jolts of suffering?*

It was then that the race, the truth about the race, began to tickle. The first thoughts, the true doubts that had to be crushed or they would end the race before it started, the first true doubts: *How the hell can I do this? How the hell can anybody do this?*

There came a time then of almost unbroken, back-breaking effort. God, it was staggering—all that had to be done.

With the realization that I knew nothing came the need to learn, and the best way to learn about running dogs—other than begging information—was to run dogs.

I ran teams constantly. At first when I met other teams I was too shy—and embarrassed about my ignorance—to talk much or ask questions. But fear quickly took over, fear that the same ignorance would lead to disaster—and I started asking.

I can remember exactly when it happened. It was in the middle of the night when I met another team head on. In the area where we were training the snow was viciously deep powder. The dog trails—hundreds of miles of them—were kept packed solid by dogs running on them, but a step off the trail could drop you armpit-deep in snow. On this night the snow off the trail was at least waist-high, and when we met I ran up to pull my team off to the side so the other musher could get past. (I was very much aware of my amateur "foreign" status—having come from "down below," or "outside"—and didn't want to inconvenience anybody.) As I approached the front of the team and reached for Cookie it brought me next to the other team's lead dog. It was a small dog, a female, and she promptly snaked in and took a chunk of my pants leg off, catching some meat along with it.

"God*damn!*" I jumped away, fell into the deep snow, and the little bitch took advantage of it by nailing me twice more, on the arm and chest, as I stumbled around in the snow. I was still clutching Cookie's harness, trying to keep her out of it. But she loved a good fight more than anything (except, perhaps, eating cats, a fact that had caused some friction between Ruth— who loves cats—and Cookie).

With a happy growl Cookie piled in, which dragged the point dogs up, and *they* jumped into it. Soon eight or nine dogs from both teams were having at it, with me on the bottom, and I wasn't all that sure I would get out of it.

"Come on, goddamnit! *Stop* this shit!" The other musher waded in, pulling dogs off me by jerking on their harnesses. "Get *out* of there, damnit!"

I rolled on my hands and knees, stood, straightened my headlamp to find myself peering at a red-bearded man with ice frozen in his beard.

"Sorry," he said. "She's bad that way—bad to start fights."

"She bit me . . ."

He nodded, his headlamp bobbing in the darkness. "Yeah, she doesn't like anybody much. I'll hold her off to the side while your team passes . . ."

He dragged the small lead dog off into the deep snow and held her in back of him with both hands while I passed. If I had felt singled out for her attention I needn't have. While he held her and I dragged my dogs past she absolutely tore his ass to pieces. It was like a meat grinder back there, shredding his clothing, spitting out bits of insulation and butt and ripping anew.

At last it was accomplished and I had passed. I stopped my sled next to his. He pulled his team out so the sleds were near each other but the dogs were heading in opposite directions and came back to his sled. His coveralls and the back of his parka hung down in shreds and his hands were dripping blood.

"I have a question," I said.

"What is it?"

"That thing is a menace. Why the hell do you keep her?"

He stared at me as if I were insane. "Christ, man, she's the best dog I've ever had. I've never seen her tug go slack . . ."

And there it was—the only absolute, the single most important thing, the be-all and end-all of running dogs on the Iditarod: a tight tug.

I did not understand it yet, did not know how important it would become; did not realize that I would live for it, die for it, fixate on it, become totally obsessed with it, eat, sleep, and dream of it.

A tight tug.

Mile after mile, hour after hour, into days and weeks and months, *thousands* of miles would pass beneath the runners while I stood on the back of the sled and stared at the tugs. And there came a time, there came in fact many times when I would gladly have taken the small bitch who tore me apart, would have paid good money for her, would have let her eat my ass off and swapped my soul for her.

Later, miles and lives later, I sat at a checkpoint and watched a man feeding his dogs. He could not get close to them without injury. They were half-wild, yellow-eyed beasts, some with hair that hung to the ground. And they hated. Not just men, not just all men—including the man who rode their sled—but all things. Other dogs, trees, the world—they simply hated. While feeding, the musher had to place the food in a bowl, then use a stick to push the bowl to where the picketed dog could reach it. In a later checkpoint these same dogs would catch a dog from another team, kill it in seconds, and start *eating* it before they could be dragged off. (In a similar story that I have not been able to verify but everybody swears is true, it is said that a woman running a team in Canada climbed into the middle of a team fight and went down and was killed and partially eaten by her dogs.) When I asked the sled driver how he harnessed them he quipped, "I had a cousin help me but he quit before the race . . ."

But they pulled.

My god, how those dogs pulled. I watched them leave a checkpoint just ahead of me, saw them churn up a small mountain like a fur-covered rocket, and would gladly have suffered injury for such a team.

Tugs, pulling, that sweet curve of power from the gangline and up over their backs became everything—more than money, love, family—more than life.

The tug.

* * *

Two things happen well before the race and they are of each other and combine to cause chaos.

First, the absolutely numbing logistical truth of the race emerges. To wit: the race, taken from a logistics standpoint, is impossible. A dog team must start in downtown Anchorage and go to downtown Nome—1,180 miles away. They must be fed a snack every hour, rested, nurtured, have booties put on their feet, fed full meals every four hours, have their harnesses replaced, and the sled they pull must be repaired. If they are injured they must be flown out and sent back to the prison in Anchorage, where the convicts will care for them until they are picked up. Food must be flown in, dropped at eighteen checkpoints across Alaska; also replacement gear, booties, spare harnesses, *different* foods for the dogs in case they get bored with the food and need a change (which happens frequently—and was the reason why I shipped sixty pounds of turkey gizzards to each checkpoint as a bonus for the team; a fact that provided some merriment when word spread around). Coupled with shipping food and gear, if by some incredible miracle a team should get to Nome, the entire team—sled, dogs, and gear—have to be crated, boxed, wrapped, taped, and flown *back* to Anchorage, as there are no roads to drive back and the thought of turning the dogs around and running back is so daunting as to be unthinkable. (There is, however, a story of an Inuit dog team that a man drove 600 miles from his village to run in a 400-mile race. He won the race, then turned around and ran his team home with the prize money.)

All of this, the enormity of the operation, the hundreds, thousands of things that needed to be done, came screaming at me at exactly the same time that a startling truth became overwhelmingly evident.

There was no more time.

Somehow it had gone. The months of training, the seemingly endless hours, the long days and longer nights had mysteriously gone and there was no time left.

And then it *all* happened. There was the thought that as the race approached things would snap into form—or at least move that way. Nothing could have been further from the truth. Indeed, everything seemed to fall apart and a frantic air dominated.

Suddenly there weren't enough booties. Six hundred had been made, sewn on an ancient Singer sewing machine. But word was the snow was bad along the trail (this meant nothing to me; I did not understand sugar snow, a granular form of crystal that is murder on dogs' feet and required constant booties). It was estimated that at least eleven hundred booties would be needed, and cloth was found in Anchorage and sewing began anew.

At the same time—and time was accelerating exponentially now—the team had to be hauled to Anchorage for the vet check. Each dog had to be checked by a veterinarian to ensure he or she was in condition to run. (One of the paradoxes of the race is that while extraordinary care is given to checking and caring for the dogs, as it should be—they are checked methodically before the race, examined by vets at each checkpoint during the race, checked for drugs or other stimulants, checked for proper feeding, checked for possible dehydration constantly—while every possible examination is made of the dogs, nothing is done about the mushers. Nobody checks the humans or the food they send for themselves—this has led in the past to such oddities as mushers running the whole race without a change of clothes, eating only Snickers candy bars for food, and thinking one set of batteries will last all the way.)

With the vet check came the need to bag supplies and ship them from the Anchorage airport and meanwhile the sled had to be virtually rebuilt, with new plastic runner shoes fastened on and every bolt or lashing examined and retightened at the same time that more booties had to be sewn and a sled bag had to be made and a dog food cooker manufactured and still *more* booties sewn and more food found and gear checked and time was gone and in a few days the dogs had to be hauled to Anchorage again for staging and the race start, and right then a man came to camp and looked at the dogs and shook his head.

"Christ, you're not going to run them like that, are you?"

A numbing fear gripped my heart. Immersed as I was in ignorance I was ready to accept anybody's opinion.

"Why—what's wrong with them?"

"They're full of it. You've got to tire them out before the race."

"Tire them—I thought it would be just the opposite. You'd want them rested."

He shook his head again. "How many dogs are you going to run?"

Rules about dogs cover many pages. You cannot add dogs—the dogs you leave Anchorage with, in harness, pulling the sled, are the dogs you must run. This is because one man had actually tried to run with two full teams—one pulling and ten spare dogs in cages on an enormous sled. It had proven disastrous—he had trouble making the first corner (something I would come to understand and sympathize with) and so came the rule about dogs having to pull. The rules state that at least seven dogs must be on a team, and not over twenty. For obvious reasons—moose attacks against teams and drivers are very common, dogfights, shoulder injuries—people try to leave with as many dogs as possible in case they have to drop some (fly them back to Anchorage). I had brought twenty dogs to Alaska but after training and running in mountains it was clear not all of them were distance-oriented dogs. I had weeded them down, found homes for those that obviously weren't going to make it, and I was going to run every dog that I thought would work out.

"Fifteen," I answered him. "I'm going to run fifteen dogs."

"No." He shook his head one more time. "You're going to run fifteen *Iditarod* dogs."

I nodded. "So?"

"They are strong, tough—hell, three of them on a sled will take you fifty miles a day. Fifteen of them, on a sled in downtown Anchorage, fresh and full of piss, is a goddamn disaster looking for a place to happen. You've got to run them, burn them down a bit so you can handle them in town."

"But the race is next week!"

"My point"—he nodded—"exactly."

Much advice is given by people who have never run, never started the race, some of it by people who have never even had dogs. It is not conceit or arrogance that causes this—simply that everybody wants so much to be *involved*. I did not know it at the time, but that was the case with this man.

Still, in a way he was right. I needed more control of the team—always, but especially in downtown Anchorage—but his method was wrong. Disastrously.

I set out to wear them down. Fifteen dogs on a sled, lightly loaded, back-to-back sixty-mile runs. To say that it didn't work would be only a half-truth.

It not only didn't work, it had the exact opposite effect. The team had become amazingly tough—bullet-proof—and the snow conditions (good, packed trail from countless teams running on them, ten-below temperatures) did nothing to tire them.

Running them on sixty-mile runs with good trail to tire them, in their condition and frame of mind, was like trying to put out a fire by pouring gasoline on it. It merely pumped them up, and by the time the clock ran out and everything came to a head and it was time to head into Anchorage for the start I had what amounted to a pack of fifteen wild dogs absolutely full of adrenalin and I knew it, could *feel* the insanity in them.

"I'm not going to get out of Anchorage alive," I told a friend.

And it proved to be just about the only time I was close to being right.

THE RACE

Pre-Race

At no time—according to Ruth, who came up to Alaska for the race itself—was the start of the Iditarod anything but completely unhinged. If there was order—and there must have been, or else the race would never have happened—it didn't show.

There was the beginning of a plan—and the idea was straightforward. Everybody who had signed up for the race brought their team to the center of downtown Anchorage on the first Saturday in March and started the race, the teams leaving at two-minute intervals.

Good enough, on the face of it—and it sounded simple. But what it *really* meant was that something on the order of twelve to fourteen *hundred* dogs had to be brought to the downtown section and staged into the start. Moreover, they had to come in two days prior to the actual start so that all the musher meetings could be attended. By this time it had become evident to even the most amateur of mushers that the dogs were vital—a preciously limited resource—and most mushers hated to leave their teams. Yet they had to for the interminable meetings.

The trail was discussed, the kind of gear allowed— much was made of snowshoes. The rules state that all mushers must carry a good artic sleeping bag, a good parka, a two-day supply of food for the dogs and humans (meat for the dogs, sometimes candy bars for the humans), booties to last for two days (it was thought that even if storms came up, the longest time between checkpoints would be two days—a thought future storms would help cause to be changed), a first-aid kit, spare batteries, an ax, and finally, a pair of snowshoes to break trail for the dogs if the snow got too deep. I had a pair of trail shoes that I used on the trapline for working in soft snow and I had brought them to Alaska for the race. They were long and comfortable and I was accustomed to using them, but they were heavier than they needed to be, and I didn't yet understand the importance of having light equipment and indeed could not have afforded new ones even if I had thought of it. (I would later seriously even consider reducing the size of the snaps hooking the tugs to the harness to lose weight.)

God, for the talk of snowshoes. I felt sorry for the race marshals and judges who stood and patiently tried to explain that what the rules meant was just a pair of snowshoes that were functional if you needed them.

One man asked for the square-inch measurement required if his body weight were 180; another asked if he was lighter and only weighed 155 could he have shoes with a smaller area, and that opened the door to what amounted to seemingly endless bickering. We needed to carry an ax, one man pointed out, but it didn't say anything about the ax having a certain length handle and could you legally carry an ax with a four-inch handle or an ax with *no* handle? From there it degenerated into weight of sled bags, food, batteries, how many ounces of this, ounces of that.

I sat in shock for much of it. I would have thought the discussion would be more on trail conditions, weather reports, bad ice—this thing with the rules (and we discussed every single one of the rules, always with somebody picking at something) was endless.

When it was at last finished we had still more talk—finally—about the trail and at the end, an impromptu briefing held for the rookies. This is a regular part of race preparation now—a briefing for the rookies—but then it was all informal and a couple of mushers who had run the race before sat and had coffee and answered questions.

My problem was I didn't know enough to have any questions. Names came at me that didn't mean anything.

Finger Lake.

Happy Canyon.

Rainy Pass.

The Burn.

Don's cabin.

It was warm in the room and we had just finished the first series of informal briefings and I hadn't slept in what felt like two months—something very close to the truth—and most of the talk drifted away from me until somebody said: "No rookie should start the Burn after dark. Not if he wants to stay sane."

I held up my hand. "What's the Burn?"

All heads swiveled, eyes locked on me, plain amazement in their faces—even the other rookies. On some of them the look changed to pity—to not know what the Burn was, at this late date, their faces said, you poor bastard.

One musher who had run the race six or seven times sighed and looked at his watch. "The Burn comes just after Rohn River checkpoint, which is just after coming down Rainy Pass and just before hitting Nikolai and the run over to McGrath." He took a sip of coffee. "The Burn is just under one hundred miles of brush and trees that were burned out in a forest fire. Because the wind blows there all the time there is usually no snow. So it's a hundred or so miles through burned and fallen logs, running on dirt and hummocks and rocks and brush. Some say it's the hardest part of the race but I don't think that—it's maybe the third hardest." He took another drink from the Styrofoam cup and smiled while he swallowed. "Everybody has a different opinion but one thing holds: it's real easy to go ass-over-balls crazy in there, and if you're a rookie, don't start it at night."

"Oh." I nodded, wishing I had kept my mouth shut. "Thank you."

"No sweat."

As luck, all bad, would have it, I would start the Burn at night, find it much worse than he had said, and go mad in about the middle of it. But I did not know that then and for the rest of that afternoon and early evening before the start of the race I sat in ignorance—if not blissful at least not as painful as it would become—and listened and tried to take notes as the mushers and volunteers described what I thought would be most important: the trail and the country we had to cross.

It was a litany of horrors.

"The trail coming down Happy Canyon is narrowed by deep snow and has two switchbacks that can't be done, so be careful."

If they can't be done, I thought, what difference does it make if you're careful? If it can't be done then that's it, isn't it? You just stop the race and go home then, right? But I said nothing.

One of the trail bosses studied a notebook for a moment. "Watch out for suckholes on the Yukon. I flew over the river yesterday and there seemed to be some bad ones in the north end."

I couldn't help myself. My hand went up. "What are suckholes?"

Another long look from everybody in the room. Clearly they all wondered how in the living hell I had managed to exist as long as I had without knowing what a suckhole was. I was less than nothing.

"Suckholes are frozen whirlpools," the trail boss told me. "Some are large enough for a whole team and driver to fall in—like a big frozen cone with an opening in the bottom that slips you into the river under the ice. The problem is that sometimes they will be covered by snow and you can't see them until you're on top of them and falling in." He took a breath. "So watch it."

I nodded, but again, the dilemma wasn't lost on me and I opened my mouth one more time. "If you can't see them how do you watch for them?"

One of the experienced mushers who had stayed for another cup of coffee sat down next to me. "There might be a little steam coming up off the open water, just like whuffs of smoke through cracks in the snow cover. Look for that. And watch your lead dogs. If they start acting funny or breaking through, get on the brake—instantly. You won't have three seconds before they all start sliding in."

He stopped. "Thank you," I said. "We don't have them in Minnesota."

He smiled, not unkindly. "There are one hell of a lot of things up here that you don't have in Minnesota."

And there, I think, lies one of the fundamental problems for rookies who come to the race from "outside." Alaska truly is wonderfully, viciously, terrifyingly, and joyously extreme. Trying to relate to what happens in the race, going across the interior with a dog team, in normal terms simply doesn't work.

"Watch for wind out by Don's cabin," a trail helper said. "It's picking up a bit." Don's cabin will turn out to be not a cabin at all but a caved-in shack that the bears tear apart in the summer. The wind "picking up a bit" will blow my lead dogs back on top of me in a snarling, fighting ball with me in the middle; will blow the sled and team and me dragging on a catch rope across the tundra off the trail for what seems like miles, tumbling and flopping; will catch me from the side and lift my eyelids from my eyeballs and drive needle-sharp points of snow into them.

"It's been a bit colder on the Yukon so take extra socks," another trail helper said. "A bit colder" will mean one man with frozen eyeballs, will mean steel bolts shearing off and frostbitten fingers and cheekbones turning black with dead flesh, will mean one man, a doctor, having to have his nose amputated because gangrene can and frequently does go hand-in-hand with frostbite.

I dutifully wrote them all down. Sentences that seem simple, almost inane, but which will prove cataclysmic in effect.

Deep snow on Rainy Pass.

Tricky ice on the Yukon and later in Norton Sound.

Some wind coming out of Old Woman Canyon on the run from the Yukon out to the Bering Sea.

Some wind in the interior.

No snow along the coast. As with the Burn, that threw me—how it was possible to run the sled without snow for the runners. It also brought out the kind of thought process that pervades outside thinking about the race. To wit: if it is bad someone will come along and fix it. Somebody, some committee, some group, will somehow fix the trail to make it usable where there is no snow, where the ice is bad, where the wind and sleet and snow hurt; Mommy will come and fix. I didn't say anything but it was there, in my thinking, that concept. But I was wrong. They do not come along and fix it. They do not help you. There is nobody out there making snow so it will be nice. Nobody to stop the wind. Nobody to hold your hand and help you over the next hill or mountain, nobody to pull you out of the cold water if you go through, nobody to do all the work of caring for the dogs. Other mushers can and often do help in emergencies. But there are only seventy or so of them, and they are spread out in a wilderness area as large as the entire eastern seaboard from Maine to the tip of Florida. It isn't exactly crowded. Effectively you and the dogs are alone.

Or, as one musher put it later when it seemed impossible to go on, "Shit, man, this is the Iditarod. If it was easy, *everybody* would run the goddamn thing."

✳ ✳ ✳

It is tempting when thinking of the race to just ignore the pre-race activities that culminate the night before the race at the official banquet. In my life I have been to many official and unofficial banquets but the one in Anchorage before the race takes all honors for both quality and length.

Attending the pre-race banquet is mandatory. If a musher does not go to the banquet dressed in mushing gear (including, for many, fur hats and parkas) and meet all the people, does not go up and draw his bib number in front of the audience, he is disqualified before the race starts. It should be a night of peace, settling the mind, getting gear and dogs ready—as should the entire last two or three days before the race. It is, instead, a night of partying, dancing, raising hell, and—for some—serious, professional drinking.

And it is a night without end. If the banquet lasted two, three hours it would be enough. It lasted virtually all night. Each musher came forward to draw his number and then stood to the microphone to thank all of his or her sponsors.

"I'd like to thank my cousin Herbie for a dog and I'd like to thank my uncle Nick for a dog and my other cousin Carl for a dog and Carl's wife's sister for 60 booties and John's wife's best friend for 125 booties and Ace Lumber for the boards to make a sled and Alaska Plywood for the wood for a dog box and . . ."

I timed one of them who was already well greased and he spoke for sixteen minutes, thanking all the people who had helped him. *Sixteen minutes,* I thought, wincing inwardly. There were seventy-four of us. Seventy-four times sixteen. I used the spoon handle to compute time on a napkin. Eleven hundred and eighty-four minutes. Just under twenty hours. I looked at my watch. It was eleven o'clock. We didn't have twenty hours—the race started in twelve. God. I thought of all that had to be done still and wondered how in hell I could do it and still get some rest. I had gone over two days without sleep and could not imagine starting the race in twelve hours without at least a catnap.

I swung around the room, looking at other tables, and saw one musher who had won the race the year before. He was face down on the table, either passed out or sound asleep, I couldn't tell. When I looked around the hall further I saw others, clearly sleeping, their heads back and mouths open, and I realized that the only rest I would get—if I got any—would have to be there at the banquet. I leaned back, closed my eyes, the noise of the banquet washed over me, and I dozed, slipping in and out, everything a soft, mental blur until it all dropped and I slept sitting in the chair, my head thrown back and mouth wide open . . .

The banquet did not last twenty hours. But it went until almost three in the morning when Ruth wiggled my arm and told me it was time to go.

We moved back to the downtown staging area, where a man had been watching the dogs as they slept in the dog boxes on the trailer. We had been given maps of the start and directions on how each team would be brought to the chutes. I studied the map for a moment (in the whole race, that map, of the first two blocks, and these directions were the only such aids given), then set to work on my gear, getting the sled ready. Ruth and the handlers offered to help but I thought it was best to do this alone now, so I would know where everything was, see that all the equipment was in order, and for that reason I was standing alone when the sun came up. Ruth and the handlers were sleeping in the truck.

It was not cold, perhaps fifteen above, and soft, and I was working by the light from my headlamp, spreading ganglines and checking each tug for the hundredth time. (I had had a nightmare repeatedly that just as I was being released in the chutes, all the tugs broke and the dogs took off running loose in Anchorage—something that would prove not far from the truth, as it happened.) The batteries had nearly gone and I was loathe to replace them yet, thinking I would start with a new set tonight, the first night of the race, and suddenly—almost in a moment—I found that the dim light from my headlamp had been replaced by a gentle golden wash that covered everything, and I turned to see the sun coming up over the mountains.

Anchorage is set like a jewel in a nest of beautiful snowcapped peaks, and the light somehow both silhouettes them and shows them at the same time, a phenomenon I will see again and again in the race. It is strikingly beautiful. Clear weather in southern Alaska is relatively rare—many stay for months and never see Mt. Denali/McKinley because of the clouds—and I stopped to study them, thinking for a moment that I should awaken Ruth and the others to see this, but I heard a soft whimper. I had been standing near the dog trailer, next to the box that held Cookie, and she was whining softly. We had become close, closer perhaps than I had ever been with another dog—or a person, as far as that goes. I often thought of her as a sister in some ways, and though she has passed away she has always been and will always be a dear friend. I knew she would not run away (I was not sure about many of the others, including Devil), so I opened the door of the dog box and reached in to ruffle her neck fur, feel her lick my hand, and I turned to say her name.

But she was not looking at me. Instead she was gazing over my shoulder at the sun coming through the mountains, and she smiled. I know how that sounds—there are some who will challenge humor or facial expressions in dogs, but they are wrong. She smiled often and she smiled then, studying the mountains, and I nodded.

"Pretty, aren't they?" And the two of us quietly watched the sun come up over Anchorage, gently enjoyed the still moment (we could not have known it but that would be the last such moment for weeks, months, years), while I buried my fingers in the thick fur of her neck and wished there was some way to bottle this, take this back to others, this beautiful stillness before the race.

Eagle River

The process of beginning the Iditarod in downtown Anchorage is so insane and so completely out of context with what the race really represents that it's almost otherworldly. Then, too, it is all phony—the whole Anchorage start is for television and audiences and sponsors. The truth is, you cannot run a dog team from Anchorage to Nome because outside of Anchorage there is a freeway system that cannot be stopped, even for something as intrinsically Alaskan as the Iditarod. The start is a theatrical event, and is treated as such by everybody.

Except the dogs.

And therein lay the problem of the start. There was much hoopla, television cameras, crowds of people, and nearly fourteen hundred dogs jammed into a short stretch of Fourth Street in the middle of the downtown section. Starting well before the race crowds gathered, loudspeakers began blaring, and dogs started barking as they were harnessed. Barking dogs begot barking dogs and soon the whole street was immersed in a cacophonous roar that made it impossible to hear anything.

Worse, the dogs became excited. And like the barking, excitement breeds on itself until dogs I thought I'd known for years were completely unrecognizable, were almost mad with eagerness. It wasn't just that they wanted to run—there simply wasn't anything else for them. Everything they were, all the ages since their time began, the instincts of countless eons of wolves coursing after herds of bison and caribou were still there, caught in genetic strands, and they came to the fore and the dogs went berserk with it.

And at least as important was that the madness was infectious, carried to the people, the handlers, the mushers—especially the rookies. No matter the plan, no matter the words of caution during briefings, what might start sensibly began to pick up speed and soon everything was imbued with a frantic sense of urgency. People who walked start to trot, then run, with dogs dragging them from trucks to get hooked into the gangline to get them ready to be taken up to the chutes.

By this time I, too, was gone, caught up in the madness of it all, so immersed in the noise and insanity that if somebody had asked my name I would not have known it. I could see only the dogs, lunging on their picket chains, crazed with excitement; feel only that same pull tearing at me, the power of it all sweeping me.

And there was a very real danger in that power, the unleashed power of fifteen dogs in prime, perfect condition suddenly being released in front of a light sled and slick plastic runners. People would be hurt; people would scratch from the race in the first five blocks with broken legs, shoulders, collarbones, concussions. Sleds would be shattered, turned into kindling, and mushers would be dragged for blocks until bystanders could grab the dogs and stop them. The power was enormous and could not be controlled. There was only two inches of snow on the street, trucked in for the start, and the sleds could not be steered or slowed; brakes would not work; snowhooks would bounce off the asphalt.

It was here that I began making rookie mistakes, two of which would prove critical to the beginning of the Iditarod for me.

Caught up in anxiety, not wishing to cause problems with the race, I harnessed my dogs too soon, way too soon, and tied the sled off to the bumper of the truck. The difficulty with this was that I had pulled number thirty-two and with the dogs tied on the side, harnessed, and ready to go, waiting to go, crazy to go—every team going up to the chutes had to be taken past my team—they had to wait. Dogs do not wait well. An old Inuit belief states that dogs and white men stem from the same roots because they cannot wait, have no patience, and become frustrated easily, and it showed mightily then.

It took two minutes per team to get them in the chutes, counted down and gone, so there was an hour delay waiting for my team to be called; an hour of slamming into harness, screaming with madness every time a team was taken past us, an hour of frustration and anxiety, an hour that seemed a day, a year.

When finally it was done, or nearly done, and the dogs were completely beyond reason and only three teams were ahead of us, six minutes before chute time, right then I made the second mistake.

I changed leaders. I had Cookie in single lead position. We had worked together for two years and she knew how to lead incredibly well and I trusted her completely. But . . .

The pre-race jim-jams took me and I started thinking of what I perceived to be reality. I had never raced before and Cookie had never raced, had never led a big team in such confusion. I began to worry that since it was all so new she would not know what to do, would not know how to get out of the chutes and line the team out down the street, would be confused about running in a race.

I had a dog that was given to me just before leaving Minnesota. His name was Wilson and I had been told that he had been in races, led in races. (I found out later it was one impromptu race, with a very small team—one dog—and it was only around a yard pulling a child.)

In microseconds the anxiousness about Cookie grew to a mountain and I could easily imagine her being released, stopping in her addled state, getting run over by the team or running into the crowd, heading off in the wrong direction—all I could see was disaster.

With less than three minutes to go I unhooked Cookie and dropped her back to point position (just to the rear of the leader) and put Wilson in the front. This all took moments and before I could think on it, wonder if I'd done the right thing, eleven or twelve volunteers came with a man who was holding a clipboard.

He noted the number on my bib, smiled and nodded. "You're next."

And volunteers took the gangline in back of each set of dogs; I unhooked them from the truck and we surged forward, the dogs nearly dragging the volunteers off their feet as we threaded into the chutes.

People talked to me. A man leaned over and said something and I nodded and smiled but I could not hear a thing over the din from the team. I also had a new sensation. Stark goddamn terror was taking me as I looked down the street over fifteen dogs and realized that this was it, that they were going to take me out hanging like an idiot on the sled.

A man leaned down with a megaphone next to my ear.

"Five!"

"Four!"

"Three!"

"Two!"

"One!"

But the dogs had watched too long, had memorized the count, and when the counter hit three and the volunteers released the team and stood off to the side they lunged, snapped loose from the men holding back the sled and I was, quite literally, gone.

I had started the Iditarod illegally—two seconds too soon.

* * *

I do not hold the record for the person coming to disaster soonest in the Iditarod. There have been some mushers who have never left the chutes. Their dogs dove into the spectators or turned back on the team and tried to go out of the chutes backwards. But I rank close.

There is a newspaper photo somewhere showing me leaving the chutes, that shows Wilson with his tongue out the side of his mouth and a wild look in his eye as he snakes the team out and away from the starting line with a great bound. (It also shows me apparently smiling; for the record the smile is not humor but the first stages of rictus caused by something close to terminal fright.)

We made almost two blocks. The distance before the first turn. Wilson ran true down the track left by the previous thirty-one teams. Until the turn. At the end of two blocks there was a hard turn to the right to head down a side street, then out of town on back trails and alleys and into the trees along the highways away from Anchorage.

I remember watching the turn coming at alarming speed. All the dogs were running wide open and I thought that the only way to make it was to lean well to the right, my weight far out to the side to keep the sled from tumbling and rolling.

I prepared, leaned out and into the turn and would have been fine except that Wilson did not take the turn. He kept going straight, blew on through the crowd and headed off into Anchorage on his own tour of discovery.

I could not stop them. The sled brakes and snowhook merely scraped and bounced off the asphalt and concrete. I tried setting the hook in a car bumper as we passed, tearing it off the car (why in god's name are they all made of plastic?), and for a space of either six blocks or six miles—at our speed time and distance became irrelevant—I just hung on and prayed, screaming "WHOA!" every time I caught my breath. Since I had never used the command on the team before it had no effect whatsoever and so I got a Wilson-guided tour of Anchorage.

We went through people's yards, ripped down fences, knocked over garbage cans. At one point I found myself going through a carport and across a backyard with fifteen dogs and a fully loaded Iditarod sled. A woman standing over the kitchen sink looked out with wide eyes as we passed through her yard and I snapped a wave at her before clawing the handlebar again to hang on while we tore down her picket fence when Wilson tried to thread through a hole not much bigger than a housecat. And there is a cocker spaniel who will never come into his backyard again. He heard us coming and turned to bark just as the entire team ran over him; I flipped one of the runners up to just miss his back and we were gone, leaving him standing facing the wrong way barking at whatever it was that had hit him.

I heard later that at the banquet some people had been speaking of me and I was unofficially voted the least likely to get out of Anchorage. Bets were made on how soon I would crash and burn. Two blocks, three. Some said one. It was very nearly true.

Back on the streets I started hooking signs with the snowhook. They were flimsy and bent when the hook hit them and I despaired of ever stopping, but at last my luck turned and the hook caught on a stop sign just right and hung and held the team while I put Cookie back in the lead and moved Wilson—still grinning wildly and snorting steam and ready to rip—back into the team.

I now had control but was completely lost and found myself in the dubious position of having to stop along the street and ask gawking bystanders if they knew the way to the Iditarod trail.

"Well, hell, sure I do. You take this street down four blocks, then cross by the small metal culvert and catch the walking path through the park there until you see the gas station with the old Ford parked out front where you hang a kind of oblique right . . ."

It is a miracle that I ever got out of town. Finally I reasoned that I had fallen somehow north of the trail and I headed in a southerly direction and when we had gone a mile or so Cookie put her nose down and suddenly hung a left into some trees, around a sharp turn and I saw sled runner marks and we were back on the trail. (As we moved into this small stand of birch and spruce I saw shattered remnants of a sled in the trees and found later that a man had cracked the whip on the turn and hit the trees and broken his leg and had to scratch. He was not the first one to scratch; there had already been two others who gave it up before getting out of town.)

I was four and a half hours getting to the first official checkpoint at Eagle River—a suburb of Anchorage—where I was met by the handlers and Ruth. We had to unhook the dogs and put them in the truck and drive on the freeway to where the race truly starts, at Knik, on the edge of the bush.

"How's it going?" Ruth asked as I loaded the dogs.

"After this it ought to be all downhill," I said. "Nothing can be as hard as getting out of town . . ."

It was a statement I would come to think of many times during the following weeks.

Skwentna

It was, strangely, quiet. And very dark, pitch dark. Clouds had come with the night, bringing the imminent threat of snow. The only light was from our headlamps and even that seemed diminished, sucked away by the thick darkness.

I was not alone. Another man, one of the other rookies, was near me. Our teams were spread out on the trail, one in back of the other, and they were also quiet. Considering their usual noisiness when near another team, their silence added to the strangeness. One dog on the other team had been taken out of harness and was lying on the snow between us. The dog was breathing, but just, and the man kneeled next to the dog. The man was crying and he wrapped his fingers in the neck ruff of the dog and held it—it was the same way I often held Cookie's neck for fun—a close, intimate gesture. As he held the fur, the dog died, and the man looked off to the side of the trail where a large form lay bulked in the snow.

"Fucking moose," he said.

I did not say anything—felt indeed that I was intruding on his grief, something I had always viewed as private—and I looked at my watch and was stunned to see that it was not yet midnight.

It was still the first day of the race.

And yet so much had happened that it seemed eons had passed; that I had somehow entered a time warp.

Not twelve hours had gone since the start of the race, and I had done everything wrong that a rookie could do.

*　*　*

The restart at Knik went fairly well. We trucked the dogs there from Eagle River and hooked them up, and were led to an unbroken line of trees and released in the order we arrived. Somebody called it "the bush," and I smiled until I found he was right—it was, suddenly, the edge of wilderness. I kissed Ruth. She was crying because she had heard the trail was very dangerous and that this would be the year a rookie would finally be killed; a grief heightened later in the race when, for two hours, I was mistakenly reported dead over the ham radio network. The handlers and volunteers took us to a narrow track that disappeared into the trees and let me go, and the team vanished out ahead of me around the turn. The sled cracked the whip, rolled, and I dragged on my face as I left the restart—and, as a matter of fact, continued to drag until an opposite turn cracked the whip in the other direction and I was flipped upright.

The mistakes started at once; little errors that led to big ones. My clothing was packed with snow from dragging, and while I was unzipping, pulling out, shaking down—all while being whipped through the woods by a dog team gone mad once more with running—I did not pay attention to the trail.

Cookie was in charge, knew how to follow the tracks, knew how to swing out so the team could clear the tight corners in the thick spruce trees and brush. I had long before, on the reaches of the trapline, learned to trust her completely, even to the point of sleeping in the sled while she covered miles of broken country and frozen lakes. I had trusted her with my life.

But this time she missed. All day had been consumed in the phony start and restart. It was late afternoon before I started again and what passed for evening while I was working the snow out of my clothing before it could melt and refreeze. While I was looking down, Cookie took a right turn at a fork, and we careened around and settled into what appeared to be the right trail, and suddenly, almost instantly, it was dark.

I fished my headlamp out of the sled bag, still letting the dogs run—it was indeed dubious that I could stop them; they were still pumped up and all but uncontrollable.

In the gathering dusk, I had not been able to see the trail well, could not tell if there were dog tracks or runner marks in the snow, and as I flicked the light, I saw that it had started to snow lightly and a dust of new powder had covered the trails so that I still could not tell if another team had come this way.

But it is no matter, I thought again, *I trust Cookie.* The fact that I did not see another team ahead of me now and then—even though I was told it is usual to see other teams until things spread out a bit more—I wrote off because I thought I had a very slow team (not necessarily true; *I* was slow, not the dogs).

Yet we were wrong, terribly wrong. What I was on was not a trail at all, was instead a snowmachine track left by a trapper working his line. Perhaps Cookie smelled meat from his packs or furs, or perhaps she just made a mistake. Whatever the reason she followed it and took me unknowingly, on the first night of the race, off into a mountain range on what I later estimated to be a 120-mile side trip—sixty out and sixty back.

Had it been a true trail, it would have been bad enough. Adding 120 miles to an Iditarod already almost impossible for me was ridiculous. But it was not a trail, was only a track, and had I not been so befuddled by the start, a lack of sleep, and my blithering ignorance, I would have known something was going desperately wrong.

It went *everywhere.* The trapper was probably looking for a place to set traps. The track would run along the side of a frozen creek for a while, then suddenly cross the creek for no apparent reason, then climb up the side of the streambed, along the edge, then drop back down into the bottom, narrowly skirting open white water along one shore, then go ripping back up out of the streambed through the trees and still farther up and away climbing the side of a mountain . . .

It was maddening. The trail made such tight turns—being controlled, as I later realized, by only the length of a snowmachine and a pulled trapline sled—that getting the dogs to snap around the corners was nearly impossible. They were constantly getting tangled, pulled off the side as the corner cut too sharply, then untangling and shooting ahead again. The dogs loved it—they viewed it as hunting or running curvy streambeds, never knowing what was around the next corner and looking forward to finding out.

I was getting destroyed. Still hoping we were on the right trail, I began to believe that perhaps it was a test. Make the first part rough so the rookies would get out sooner. I became angry—vowed to take revenge on whoever laid out the trail—and decided that they wouldn't be able to stop me. The rougher it got the harder I worked until, finally, I was whipped.

We had come up a mountain ten or fifteen miles, in a narrow canyon, and the trail came into an opening, ran up to a nearly vertical rock face, and stopped. Dead.

Cookie stood there for a moment, looking up the face of the cliff as if wondering if she should drag the team up. Then she turned and looked over her shoulder at me, waiting, the question all over her body.

"Hell, I don't know . . ."

I set the hook in the snow and walked up to stand next to her, felt her tail slapping my leg. Initially it seemed the trail simply ended at the cliff, the tracks all but covered by the rapidly falling snow. But when I kneeled down and brushed the new snow away I saw that it had been a snowmachine and that the rider had jumped off here and turned it around manually and headed back down the same trail he'd come up.

I knew then. Knew that it was the wrong trail and that I had to go back. I grabbed Cookie by the top of her harness and turned her back around on the trail, lined her up, and she pulled the rest of the team out. I caught the sled as it whipped around, jerked the snowhook out, and started back down the mountain.

That was when I saw the extent of the damage. Had it been just me it would have been bad enough. I now had to return on the snowmachine track, find the original Iditarod trail in what was fast becoming a blizzard, then move to the next checkpoint—a village called Skwentna—a full day and a half later than I had expected to arrive.

But it was worse, far worse. As I turned and started back down the mountain I saw pinpoints of light, dozens of them, working the trail coming toward me, flicking here and there through the snow.

There were twenty-seven teams coming at me. The team in back of me had followed Cookie's smell, added to it, and the other teams had followed, each adding their smell and tracks until the fake trail seemed more true than the real one.

It was a nightmare. As I wound down on the narrow trail, the snow coming heavier all the time, the wind picking up and the dogs still full of piss and vinegar, it turned into something very close to war.

As one team would meet another team head on—not a good situation on the widest and best of trails, let alone this narrowed snowmachine track—the dogs would bristle.

"On by! On by!" we would yell, trying to verbally push the teams past each other. It rarely worked. Hair would go up with the "it's-my-trail-no-it's-*my*-trail" look and somebody would bump somebody and the crap would hit the fan. In an instant two dogs would be into it, two would get two more, four would get four more, and before we could get off the runners and up to the dogs there would be a thirty-dog fight.

Chaos reigned. In my life I have never before or after spent such a violent three hours. Soon we had three teams meeting three teams—eighty-, ninety-dog fights.

At one point there were six teams bottlenecked on the trail. Six teams tangled over each other, jammed into the tiny space, and when that was somehow cleared and finally it seemed that all the teams were lined out I heard a yell in back of me—"Look out!"—and turned to see the night, the whole night and darkness, suddenly move and come at me.

I had time to think the word *moose*. And that was it. It was on me. A cow of five or six hundred pounds, a dark hole in the trees at the side of the trail that caught no light, didn't seem to have form, detached itself from the background and ran over me like a train.

I had been attacked by moose before, while training, and had shot some of them when I had a gun. But not this suddenly and not this completely. I hadn't brought a gun on the race—because I didn't have one and had been using a borrowed weapon while train-ing—but it wouldn't have done me much good if I had. She was just there, instantly, and I was down. She hit me twice with her feet—thudding kicks—and then left me. I rolled and stood, grabbed at the sled and pulled myself up, and turned to see the moose swing to her left and hit the team in back of me.

That is what saved me, the team following. All of the teams I met except one turned as I came to them and went down ahead of me. This one team had met and passed me before turning and was following me as we made our way down.

The moose took the team, hit the leader head on and stomped the dog into the snow, then stayed on it, kicking at the downed dog and snaking out at the point dogs with her hooves.

She was almost not there. Somehow the light from my headlamp didn't reflect from her; it was like watch-ing a malevolent shadow hit the team. And I couldn't think, Moose . . . Do . . . Something.

The ax. I had an ax on the sled—it was manda-tory—and I reached for it, though god knows what I thought I was going to do. Hitting her with an ax would do nothing but piss her off. But as I reached there was a flat crack and a flash of light, then another and another and another.

Five times. The man on the other sled had a hand-gun and he had come running forward and shot the moose through from the side, each bullet striking her in the chest, each one hitting her solidly.

Still she did not go down. She kicked at the dog more, at the man, then turned to her left, took another

kick at the point dogs—one was down but would recover—and walked off into the snow and sank and
died there.

Twenty seconds hadn't passed since she hit me,
and it was over. With the moose gone the man turned
to his leader and kneeled in time to hold the dog's neck
while it died and to say, "Fucking moose."

That's when I looked at my watch and found that
it was still the first official twenty-four-hour period of
the race, and had I taken stock of my progress I would
probably have scratched. Because of my side trip I was
actually starting the race now with a minus mileage.
Along with all the teams that had followed me, we
were now effectively restarting the race with an extra
120 miles tacked on. It wasn't 1,180 miles any more;
it was 1,300.

Add to that the violence—the hours of dogfights,
the moose taking the lead dog on the team where the
man now kneeled crying softly—and had I been at all
sensible or objective I would have pulled the pin. I
have often wondered what would have happened to me
had I quit then. I probably would not have stayed in
dogs, would have gone on to other, saner lives . . .

But I was confused. There was the lack of sleep.
Except for the forty drooling winks I had stolen at the
banquet the night before—life before? ages before?—
I had not slept in nearly three days. My brain was so
fried with sleep deprivation that I was on the edge of
hallucinating (and indeed, had I known that this was
nothing, that I would probably never sleep a full night
again, there would have been more fuel for scratching)

and the ability to think lucidly or objectively was completely gone.

Then there was the race itself. I was no longer of that other world—the non-race world. The normal world. (Here again, had I known the altering was permanent I might have stopped.) Work, living, family, society—none of it seemed real. All that was real was here—standing in falling snow next to a dead moose leaning over a man who was crying for a dead lead dog. Had somebody told me then of other perceived realities—of car payments or light bills or school programs or wives or children—I would have thought him absurd.

And finally, there was Alaska—the seductive, wonderfully magnificent deadly beauty of the place.

Dawn was coming while we stood there. As the gray light came it grew colder—though not below zero; mean cold would not come until we were in the interior—and the cold stopped the snow, somehow moved all the clouds away, and as the sun came up it illuminated the peaks in the Alaska Range. Because we were still high up and away from the river leading to the first checkpoint at Skwentna, everything was visible; all of southern Alaska seemed to show.

It probably wasn't sudden, but it seemed so. It seemed that one second I was looking down with my headlamp glow at the pietà-like scene of the man holding the dead dog's head in his lap and the next I was looking up to see all of Alaska before me, caught in a pink-gold light. Far below, stretching away to the right, I could see the Susitna River, and as the light grew stronger I could make out small moving figures and I realized they were teams winding up the river as it looped back and forth. Miles away, little dots were moving along in the middle of the frozen river and I looked down at the man and the dead dog and coughed.

"What do you want to do?" I felt at least partially responsible. If I hadn't taken the wrong trail he wouldn't have followed; if he hadn't followed he wouldn't have been there for the moose to jump on. (And why had she waited for all the teams to pass? Why until this one team?)

He looked up. "I don't know. I'm not sure I have another leader."

I nodded. I had Cookie. Wilson would run in front but I wouldn't call it leading. Not after the debacle in Anchorage. I understood depending on one leader and suddenly felt a cold spot in my shoulders, down the middle of my back. Cookie. One dog. What if the moose—I would later come to call them all "fucking moose" as many others had done—what if the moose had jumped Cookie. Killed Cookie. I looked to her quickly, frightened, but she was sitting and watching me quietly, waiting for me to pull the hook.

"Will your team follow me?" Sometimes a team will follow another as long as they can see it—the chasing instinct is so strong.

He thought, frowning. "Maybe. I've never done it without Thor." He wiped his eyes. "Maybe we could tie a rope back from your sled and pull them out, get them started."

I thought on this. The rules were quite explicit. No team could pull another; no dogs could be moved from one team to another. Penalty was disqualification for both teams. On the other hand, who in hell would see us?

An idea hit me. "Let's try this. I'll put some meat on a rope and drag it, see if they'll follow the smell of it . . ."

Probably still illegal. But I could pull the meat up quickly if we saw anybody and the truth was I couldn't leave him here. If his team wouldn't move he would be stuck in a side canyon. He was at the back of the string of teams. To just leave him here alone . . .

And it worked. We wrapped his dead leader carefully in the sled bag on his sled and I took a piece of beaver meat which I tied to a long rope I used for tying off the leaders. (I didn't need it again; it went along with the spare snowhook, spare snaps, spare clothing, spare-almost-everything-but-the-kitchen-sink. I had near-terminal rookie bulge on my sled, and later would start shedding it at checkpoints to lessen weight.)

I headed out, pulling the meat, and his team followed. There was a problem at first because his dogs were nearly half a mile an hour faster than mine and he kept running up on me and having to stop. But within a mile he hooked one of his dogs—which had kept trying to look forward over the others—up on the front end and it took the lead and he passed me, thanking me for the help, moved on ahead, and left me alone.

To see the beauty. By this time we had run back down off the phony trail and returned to the correct track on the river. It was full daylight as well, midmorning, and all the clouds had blown away to reveal a clear blue sky and the panorama of a white range of mountains spread out in front of me. They were still well away—I would have to go through two check-points to get to them—but they were massively tall and looked huge even in the distance and so striking that I had gone perhaps five miles on the river before it dawned on me that they really represented the first true barrier in the race.

We would have to cross the mountains to get into the interior.

And as I ran through the day and the mountains became larger the task seemed more daunting. A phrase had started in my mind a month or so before the race when a musher who had, in fact, won the race took me out on a test run to see if I could at least start the race. At that time you did not have to qual-ify, as you do now, with five-hundred-mile or two-hundred-mile races; the only requirement was that three mushers who had finished the race sign a form saying they thought you could hold yourself together. (This made for some interesting runs; some got their forms signed over a beer and the result was people trying to run the race who barely knew how to har-ness dogs.) This particular musher said he would sign the form, but only if I ran dogs with him so he could see how I worked. We took off on a three-day run after I glibly (and, I might add, mistakenly) quipped to him, "Make it worse than the race so I won't be sur-prised."

I should have kept my mouth shut. At one point on the edge of a canyon wall he flipped his sled upside down, wrapped rope around the runners so they wouldn't slide, unhooked his dogs and pretty much free-fell down to a frozen river below. It was then the phrase came into my mind, while wrapping rope around my own runners and dropping (with my eyes closed) off the edge:

"If one person can do it, another person can do it."

It was not stunningly revelatory—but simple, perhaps stupidly so. But I had used it often in training after getting to Alaska and started to think it now on the river heading for the mountains. (I did not know it then, of course, but within four days it would become even more important; would become a mantra for me, would as a matter of fact become something I would scream to myself when the "task" became seemingly impossible.)

I nearly missed the checkpoint at Skwentna. Considering that it was a village located on a river, with airplanes landing and taking off, eighteen or twenty teams scattered on the ice, and a diesel generator bellowing constantly, this would have been something of a record. But I ran all day looking at the mountains and didn't get there until after dark and by then the lack of sleep was causing serious problems, as was the almost searing tension of getting ready for and starting the race and the constant thought all day that I would have to somehow get over this enormous range of mountains—the highest range in North America.

I was, consequently, in a trance state, my eyes open but my brain most definitely turned off, and I started past the checkpoint, would have passed except that Cookie took over and turned on a side trail at the last moment to bring us in to the checkpoint and a pile of food bags waiting for us.

Somebody, a volunteer, held a clipboard out to me and I signed in. It was a woman and she smiled and asked me something.

"What? I'm sorry, I can't hear right . . ."

She nodded. "I understand. Would you like to sign out at the same time and get it all done now?"

At each checkpoint it is necessary to sign in and sign out to show you have been there. Most mushers just signed in and out at the same time so when they got ready to leave they wouldn't have to run around trying to find the checker. It saved a lot of time and effort, but I was so fried I didn't understand what she meant.

"Here, just sign . . ." She held the clipboard out again, guided my hand with the pen, and I signed.

"Thank you," I said.

"Do you like the race so far?"

I looked at her, trying to find sarcasm, but she was serious; she really wanted to know. And I thought of how to answer her.

I had gotten lost, been run over by a moose, watched a dog get killed, saw a man cry, dragged over a third of the teams off on the wrong trail, and been absolutely hammered by beauty while all this was happening. (It was, I would find later, essentially a normal Iditarod day—perhaps a bit calmer than most.) I opened my mouth.

"I . . ."

Nothing came. She patted my arm and nodded. "I

understand. It's so early in the race. There'll be more later to talk about . . ."

And she left me before I could tell her that I thought my whole life had changed, that my basic understanding of values had changed, that I wasn't sure if I would ever recover, that I had seen god and he was a dog-man and that nothing, ever, would be the same for me again, and it was only the first true checkpoint of the race.

I had come just one hundred miles.

Finger Lake

Somehow it became night again without my planning on it.

I had remained at the Skwentna checkpoint for four hours, resting the dogs. I did not rest. I spent the entire time checking the dogs' feet—there were sixty of them and I had seen others doing it so I thought it must be time for me to do it as well. Except for cursory examinations while running, I had not as yet checked them in detail. Their feet were fine but I diligently spread their paws and looked between their toes. (Devil, as might be imagined, did *not* want me to look at his feet—a criticism he shared physically so that I had to spend part of the four hours sewing up the sleeve of my parka.) With that done, dog food cooked and placed warm in the coolers to carry on the sled and snack them, dogs watered, shoulders rubbed, two harnesses mended that had been torn in the fighting during the night, I sat on the sled just in time to get up and leave. At some point in training somebody had told me the way to rest the dogs was to watch them and when the worst—i.e., most tired—dog rose from sleep, stretched, and started to make a new bed, they had had enough rest.

It took three hours and forty-seven minutes for Max—I considered him my weakest link—to rise and begin to make a new bed. I had already packed the sled and when Max moved I stood (albeit slower than I had been rising, though still faster than I would later rise, when I couldn't get up at all) and thought to get the other dogs up.

As it happened the act was unnecessary. The other dogs had finished resting and when Cookie saw me stand she got up as well, shook, and that made the team get up. I had unhooked their tugs, leaving their collars hooked to the gangline so they could sleep un-fettered, and as I went down the line rehooking their tugs and petting each dog, they became excited. Before I was finished they were slamming into the harnesses wanting to go and I barely caught the sled when they blew the hook (jerked the snowhook out of the packed snow/ice on the river) and roared past me.

We ran all day in sunshine and peaks. I had left the checkpoint at the same time as another musher but his team was slower than mine—one of the few—and soon I was running alone again.

The country remained stupendous—and would for the rest of the race. Clear skies and bright sun set off the snow on the mountains and made them seem almost alive with brightness. The trail wound up rivers and across lakes, onto other rivers, always slightly up, until the sun was gone and it was dark.

As with almost the entire race I had absolutely no idea where in the hell I was. There was a trail, dog and sled prints on the trail, and I assumed we were going the right direction.

The next checkpoint was a trapper's cabin at a place called Finger Lake. I knew that. But I did not know how far I had come nor how far there was yet to go, and I wondered if I should stop and rest the dogs again.

Instead I watched them. They did not seem tired, and certainly did not want to stop. I had tried once to get them to stop long enough for me to take a piss and finally gave up and did it while the sled was moving, messing the sled, the trail, and my clothing in the process. (Not that it mattered. By this time, what with bloody meat, dogs pissing on my leg to "mark" me, and continually wiping foot ointment off my hands, I looked and smelled like a walking charnel house.)

So I let them run through the day and it seemed that I looked down into the sled bag sometime in late afternoon and when I looked up it was dark. This would happen to me often—and I have since found that it happened to others as well—a suspension of time, or rather a blocking out of major passages. I know I functioned. The food went down in the coolers, so I had been snacking the dogs. Some of them were wearing booties, which meant I had worked on their feet. I had taken my headlamp out of the sled bag and put it on, hooked up the batteries, and had the cone of light going out over the team but could not, truly, re-member any of it.

It was dark, but not quite completely. There were no clouds so if I flicked my light off the stars shone, and I did this. Early on, while running the trapline, I had learned the dogs ran well in the dark, could see better than I could see, and had found in training that often the light from the headlamp threw them off. It made shadows that changed distances and sometimes caused them to step wrong—the way it feels when you expect a step on a stairway and there isn't one.

I ran in the dark this way, trusting Cookie to see the trail, for another period of time—a half-hour, hour, more—and the next time I looked up the dogs had stopped and we were at the Finger Lake check-point.

In some ways it would prove to be a model for night checkpoints. There were teams in various stages of preparation, some sleeping, some sleds being packed, some leaving. Here and there dogs barked, whined to leave, but mostly it was silent as mushers' headlamps swept back and forth across the snow. Already much of the urgency of the race had dissipated; this was the "back end," the slower teams, the rookies, the people who would never finish and some who would only after learning more about themselves and dogs. Because of my side trip we were all nearly a day in back of the leaders already and most realized that catching the front end—where there were stellar names like Butcher, Swenson, Mackey (who will win)—was al-ready impossible. No rookie could seriously think of winning—not on the first race—but some would still try and they were leaving even as I arrived, pushing their teams out the back side of the checkpoint.

I turned and looked back where I had come in, saw that I had been running across a lake, and climbed up the shore of the lake to a flat area near a small log cabin. There were lights in the window of the cabin, the flat-white glare of a Coleman lantern, beaming out but rapidly absorbed by the black night.

As I watched, the door of the cabin opened suddenly inward, slamming, and two men boiled out into the snow fighting. Or rather one was fighting, slamming the other with what appeared to be a saucepan, or a cast-iron frying pan, and the other one was ducking and running with his hands over his head.

"And *stay* the fuck out!" the man with the pan yelled. He then turned and went back into the cabin, slamming the door in back of him.

The other man—a musher clad in parka and cold-weather pants—walked past me. He was laughing.

"All I wanted was a cup of coffee," he said, shaking his head. "Son of a bitch went nuts . . ."

"Why . . ." I started but didn't finish because he was out of hearing range. It didn't matter. I had already learned that if you asked questions about events in the race you only got answers that led to more questions until, finally, there couldn't be an answer based in logic. For some reason the man in the cabin had not wanted the other man to have a cup of coffee. That was it. In an upside-down way it made sense—or as much sense as anything in the race—and I turned as a checker came up to me with a clipboard. It was a young man—probably twenty-five or so. But I was forty-three and he seemed much younger. Not over thirteen.

"How is it going?" he asked.

I looked at him as I had looked at the woman checker back in Skwentna and thought of all the things I could or could not say and I shook my head, my head-lamp sweeping back and forth across his face, and I told him the truth. "I haven't got a clue."

He nodded. "That's about par for the course." He pointed. "Food sacks are over in that pile; pull your team up in there where the straw beds are."

"Straw beds?"

"Yeah. One of the mushers shipped a bale to each checkpoint. He's gone out already. You might as well use his straw."

I had not thought of that, of sending beds. I had run trapline dogs and they simply made beds in the snow—the thickness of their guard hair (the dense layer of fur that covers their body beneath the coat you actually see—so packed that even water cannot get through it; it's like wearing an inch of Styrofoam) protected them from the cold. But in a very real and true sense the dogs are the athletes of the Iditarod and de-serve every consideration, every aid. I should have thought of straw beds, I said to myself, and began to wonder how many other things I should have thought of doing.

As it happened, the dogs ignored the straw. I ran them into the same place as the other team had oc-cupied, fed them the last of the food in the thermos coolers on the sled, pulled off the used booties and ex-amined feet, and let them rest while I went for the food bags. Most of them peed on the straw, then curled up off to the side in the snow.

This time they rested a full five hours. I still did not sleep. One of the other mushers told me that he had experienced something called razor snow that made almost microscopic cuts along the top edge of each dog's toe just where the bare pad starts to be covered by fur. I was still driven almost completely by fear and ignorance—primarily fear *of* my ignorance, that it would cause damage or harm to the dogs—and any rest I might have had in the Finger Lake checkpoint was given over to studying toes.

I found the food sacks, fired up the Coleman stove I was using for a dog food cooker—noticing all the while that the "real" mushers had specially made cookers that did the work on half the fuel in a fourth the time—and heated meat to put in the coolers. I had sent meat patties mixed with cheese for myself, precooked but naturally frozen brick hard. They were in plastic bags and I put two of them on top of the dog meat to thaw out while I went from dog to dog, toe to toe, checking for the hairline cuts from the "razor snow." Most of the dogs were asleep by this time—they seemed to drop instantly into a deep sleep—and as I crouched over each one it would hold up a foot without awakening so I could examine the pads. As I put one foot down it would hold the other up, still breathing evenly, sound asleep. All except for Devil, of course, who objected to me touching his feet by taking a shot at me. It was only halfhearted—a quick snap that barely drew blood—and I wondered again if our relationship was improving.

When I had finished their feet—carefully scrutinizing each toe on each foot of each dog—they were already rested and it was nearly time to go. I went to put the hot meat in the thermos containers and saw that my meat patties had thawed and sunk into the dog meat and I dragged them out but hesitated.

I was starving but the dog meat they had sunk into was essentially made of something called "slumps." These are unborn calves inside of cows that are taken to the slaughterhouse. While the cow herself can be used for human food the slumps cannot. They are ground up and sold to dog food companies frozen in fifty-pound boxes.

They use a very coarse setting on the grinder when they process the slumps, and they grind them whole. Consequently, some strange things show up in the meat: large patches of skin with soft hair still attached; whole, small feet; and often a complete eyeball, all floating around in the mix when the meat is heated and poured into the containers.

Having my own food fall into this mixture went a long way to curbing my appetite. I snatched the packets out, but the plastic-seal bags had broken open, and some of the slump meat had mixed with my own meat.

I paused, hung on the edge for half a minute, the steam from my breath boiling in the glare of my headlamp like smoke.

The logic went like this:

Slumps were gross. I could not personally eat a slump.

But the dogs loved slump meat.

The dogs did very well on it—remained healthy, got fat; their coats shined.

I was very hungry.

If it was good for the dogs, could it be that bad for me?

I was *very* hungry.

If it was good for the dogs, and I was becoming something very like a dog, could it *possibly* be bad for me?

And so I ate the meat patties, although as a last gasp of refinement I did not eat the corner of the patty that touched my fingers.

It may seem somewhat irrelevant—all this over two meat patties—but it became important because in a very real sense, it was the crumbling of the last barrier between me and the dogs. In some primary ways, I had held on to being, if not normal, at least human, held on to thinking of myself in human terms.

From this point on there was no separation. It was not me driving the sled and the dogs pulling me.

It was us. It was we—an almost glorious *we*. As the barrier dropped and I joined them, I literally stopped thinking in human terms. By the end of the first week, I had virtually stopped talking to people. If I cut my hand, I rubbed dog ointment on it and went on. If I was cutting or heating a piece of meat I knew the dogs would like, I salivated and finally tasted it. If the day was warm—above zero—and I stopped to rest the team, I automatically put them in the shade because I felt, no, *knew* they would be more comfortable there. If the day was cold and windy, I looked for a sheltered spot open to the sun and out of the wind. So did others, of course, especially the ones who were good—Butcher, Swenson—but this was more than just aping them. I had actually started to "think dog."

And it all began, though I didn't know it yet, that night at the Finger Lake checkpoint.

When the dogs' rest cycle ended, it was just coming on daylight, a faint glow spreading across the lake in the direction we had come.

I had been sitting on the sled for a moment—we had been going constantly now for over thirty-six hours, and my legs were on fire—and Cookie turned to watch the day come (I never saw her sleep through a sunrise). I stood and that made the rest of the dogs rise, and we left the checkpoint.

Rainy Pass

On the way out the back side of the Finger Lake checkpoint area, one of the mushers yelled at me as I passed.

"You're leaving now?"

I nodded. "They want to run . . ."

"I'm waiting until dark."

I hit the brake. The dogs didn't stop, but it slowed the sled enough for me to ask, "Why?" Dark was a good eleven hours away—too long to rest.

"I don't want to be able to see Happy Canyon when I do it . . ."

And I was gone.

❋ ❋ ❋

In the pre-race briefing, we had been told in general about some of the more difficult hardships of the race—the mountains, the interior, the cold.

At that time, someone had momentarily mentioned Happy Canyon. We were told that it lay between Finger Lake and Rainy Pass—comparable to stating that New York City lies between Boston and Washington, D.C.—and that it might prove difficult because of deep snow. Or something. I had written it down but had forgotten what I'd written.

We were not told that it was a near-vertical drop down a cliff, nor that it came soon after Finger Lake, when the dogs were still rested and fresh.

I was doing something in the sled—tightening a lashing—and I looked up to see the front end of the team suddenly drop off the edge of the world.

The morning had dawned clear, but a wind had come up, blowing new snow in swirling clouds. I could not at first see where the dogs had gone because of this, but as I rapidly approached the drop point, watching each set of dogs drop out of sight, the wind eddied and momentarily cleared, and I got my first true look at Happy Canyon.

I am not religious but I think I would have prayed had there been more time. Spread out below me, as far as I could see, was an enormous canyon. The far side seemed miles away and the river down below a tiny line in the middle.

"Shit . . ." I had time for the one word (I was told later this was the most used word when confronting Happy Canyon) and then the sled, pulled by the now falling team, came to the drop-off.

I honestly do not know how I made it. Later, I was speaking to an Englishman who had run the race, and in typical British understatement, he said, "It's rather like falling, isn't it?"

Plummeting would be more the word. There was something approximating a ledge-trail that went down to an impossibly abrupt switchback, but the trail didn't matter.

Cookie, realizing that to survive she would have to stay ahead of the suddenly falling team, sled, and musher, said to hell with the trail and jumped off the edge, aimed straight down. The team, used to following her blindly, jumped off after her.

I grabbed the handlebar of the sled with both hands and hung on, dragging on my stomach as we careened, flopped, rolled, and tumbled some five hundred feet down to the frozen river below.

I would like to say that because I kept my wits about me and was cool in the face of a crisis, I used my body as a living sled drag, which kept the sled from running over the dogs, and through a series of delicately performed maneuvers, we came smoothly to a stop on the river ice below.

I would *like* to say that, but it would be a lie. While in reality that is exactly what happened, it was all accidental. As soon as we started down, I closed my eyes. I may have screamed, as two mushers who were on the ice repairing broken sleds said, but I can't remember doing so. When I opened them, I was lying on the river ice, the dogs were lined up in front of me perfectly, and the sled—wonder of wonders—was upright and all the gear intact.

Off to the side, the two mushers stood clapping

softly. One of them smiled and nodded. "Far out—I'm going to do it that way next year."

I stood, shook the snow from my clothing, and shrugged. "I didn't know any other way to play it."

"Right."

"Dumb luck . . ."

At that he nodded and was going to say more except that we heard a bellow and turned to see what appeared to be a lumber yard exploding as the next team came over the edge. Gear, bits of sled, dogs, man, odds and ends of clothing all came down in a roiling mass of barks and screamed curses.

I set my hook and helped the other two men catch the dogs and relocate the gear. The musher, a short-set man who had run the race several times, nodded and smiled at me. "Don't you just *love* this son of a bitch of a race?"

And I was taken aback to realize that he truly meant it—he really loved the race. Here was a man who had run the race several times, had never won, never even been in the money (they pay down twenty places), and he truly loved the race.

I mumbled something to him and lined my team out and left. Had I thought on it, considered my own feelings, I would have recognized that I was coming to be the same way. The race was already becoming an entity to me—becoming more than a sum of its parts—was becoming The Iditarod.

But I had other thoughts—mostly of apprehension. While very little had been said about Happy Canyon— which had nearly finished me—*everybody* had something to say about the horrors of the next stretch: Rainy Pass.

* * *

It didn't seem possible. After Happy Canyon I began the run for Rainy Pass and entered one of those periods when nothing could go wrong. The trail was well packed and fast, the steep climb areas seemed flat—we fairly flew.

All the horror stories seemed to be just that—stories. The idea of the run seemed difficult. We had to cross the Alaska Range (Mt. Denali/McKinley is in the range and is sometimes called the American Everest). And all the pre-race jitter talk *said* how horrible it was; one story even told of finding a man impaled and dead on his broken handlebar back in the old days of dog freighting when they hauled freight sleds over Rainy to supply the mines in the interior.

But it was greased, dead-easy. We loped into the checkpoint on top of the mountain at Rainy Pass Lodge without even breathing hard, the dogs full of piss and vinegar.

There was a small lodge/cabin there and fifteen or twenty teams were scattered around in the snow in different stages of readiness.

I let the team run into the checkpoint, jammed the brake down, slammed the hook into the snow with a dramatic flourish, and stepped up to the checker to sign in.

"How's it going?" It was the same young woman who had been the checker at Skwentna. There is a volunteer Iditarod "air force," several people with private planes, who fly checkers and vets from one checkpoint to the next in a leapfrog fashion. Dozens, hundreds of volunteers are still needed and used, but the leapfrogging does help some.

"I thought Rainy Pass was supposed to be hard," I said, not without some cockiness. "Hell, it was a piece of cake." (I had overlooked my near disaster in Happy Canyon, but on reflection I thought it might be like they say about childbirth pain, the bit that states something about forgetting the pain when it's over. Ruth says it must have been a man who said that, and she would like to suggest—in as delicate a manner as possible—that he try passing a watermelon, whole, before he makes such statements again.)

In any event, the checker—who is young and clear-eyed—knows a great deal more than I do. She gently put a hand on my arm.

"It's not the up part of Rainy that's hard," she said sweetly. "It's the down part."

"Oh," I answered. "Well, I *knew* that, but everybody said the up part was hard, too."

She shook her head. "No. It's the down part you've got to watch. Especially the Gorge."

I had heard talk about Dalzell Gorge but it all seemed unreal—like rumors in the army. Most of it I had discounted because it sounded frankly ridiculous and too far-fetched to be true.

The truth was no matter how hard it was, Dalzell Gorge was only a twenty-mile stretch at the bottom of Rainy Pass, leading out of the foothills onto the river and almost directly into the Rohn River checkpoint.

I had come two hundred and more miles already, plus several hundred in training, and to worry about a short twenty-mile segment seemed patently ridiculous.

I was wrong and the innocent, wide-eyed checker was absolutely correct.

It was the down part of Rainy that was the worst.

Dalzell Gorge
and the Burn

I couldn't . . . quite . . . get my brain to work. Somebody was talking, loud, verbally shaking me.

". . . . stand . . .?"

It didn't make any sense. I hadn't the slightest idea of where I was or what was happening.

"Goddamnit, can you stand up? I'm getting my ass torn in half here . . ."

I opened my eyes. Everything was white, blank, bright. I closed them, opened them once more, focused. I was staring into snow, inches from my eyes, snow reflecting the intense glare of the sun.

Why am I lying down, I thought—why sleep in the daytime?

"Goddamnit, can you stand *up*?"

The voice was louder, mixed in with the pain that was now becoming evident. My head felt like it was coming off, there was a distinct ringing in my ears, and as the head pain made me more aware and awake, I realized it wasn't just my head. My whole body was racked—felt literally like I'd been riding inside a cement mixer.

Dalzell Gorge.

There. It came that way—just the words. The Gorge, Dalzell Gorge. The Down Part.

"Listen, goddamnit—either you stand and help me or I'm letting your team go . . ."

I rolled to my other side—the pain in my chest almost made me scream—and looked up. A musher was holding the handlebar of my sled. My team was aimed down an icy trail that ran along the edge of a rushing, boulder-strewn stream. Headed into the stream, pulling off at an angle, his team lunged and barked. He had his left arm hooked through my handlebar, his right one hooked through his own, and he was right. The dogs were threatening to pull him apart. If he let my team go, they would take off and leave me . . . where? Somewhere in the gorge. If he let his own team go, they would pile into the water and head downstream to god knew where.

I rose to my hands and knees, clawed up at the handlebar of my sled, and pulled myself up, and in what can only be called a massive overstatement, I said, "All right—I've got them."

Whereupon he let go.

I did not in any way "have" them. They promptly shot off down the trail, both my feet blew out from beneath me, and I dragged after them on my face—a position I was, admittedly, getting quite good at.

It was, I remembered now, how I had done Dalzell Gorge so far.

I had left the lodge at the top of Rainy Pass in the morning after a night of "rest," trying to keep the dogs (who were decidedly untired) from fighting with the other teams. Devil had come to love the Iditarod and viewed the whole race as something of a traveling meat market. While the other dogs seemed to love fighting, Devil thought of it as a means to an end: first you fought, then your genetic codes and memories kicked in and you ate the other dog. I had seen him try to apply this process to dogs while he was fighting, actually getting an ear and swallowing it whole in the middle of a fight. He tried this during the night at Rainy Pass Lodge. All the teams were in a relatively small area, and Devil several times dragged the whole team with him in his quest for food.

It made for a long six-hour rest period and as soon as Max stood up and shook, I hooked up the tugs and we pulled out.

I was beyond tired. Days and nights without sleep had put me into a dreamlike state. But as the sun came up through the peaks, the beauty quickly dispelled the exhaustion.

The lodge was in a depression, any view partially blocked by the surrounding rise of land. But within half an hour the team pulled the sled out and up and I was treated to the spectacle of a new sun front-lighting snowcapped peaks in all directions. We were well above timberline and without trees the peaks were so clean and pristine they seemed dipped in sugar.

The lodge itself was not at the summit of Rainy Pass, and we climbed for several miles on the sides of mountains to gain the last bit.

The summit of the trail lay between two peaks— they seemed so close you could throw a rock to them— and started down.

But I had been given wrong information, or so it seemed. The "down part" was tame—a gentle grade that led away from the summit on good, packed trail.

The trail went across a tipped plain, perhaps two miles, gradually dropping all the way, and then disappeared around the side of a large rock outcropping on the right.

I thought of slowing the dogs. It was about zero degrees, no wind, clear and a little warm for them to run. But they were having such a ball loping—almost wide open—that I thought what the hell, let them run. If this was all Dalzell Gorge had to offer in the way of hardships, it would be a milk run. Hell, I thought, I'd be out the bottom in an hour and a half at this rate.

As the dogs approached the point where the trail disappeared, I heard a sound, or thought I did, and I turned away momentarily just as the dogs turned the corner; a second, no more.

When I turned back, I was struck dumb, turned to stone in horror.

The Gorge lay below and before me. A narrow passage with a rushing stream in the middle that dropped, crashing down through huge boulders and jagged rocks. There was no trail but an ice ledge that ran along one side (it would switch to the other side later over a "bridge" made from a single log only wide enough for one dog at a time and one sled runner). It was not a trail so much as a chute, and might have been passable with a walking team under close control.

I hit it wide open. Trying to use the brake on the sheer ice of the ledge to slow the team was absolutely fruitless. I took one stab at it, took another quick—horrified—look at the gorge yawning down before me, and then all hell broke loose.

Either an arm of scrub brush or a rock sticking out caught me a glancing blow on the side of the head. I remember grabbing at a piece of rope I had tied to the handlebar as a last-minute catch rope and then I was gone, swept off, dragging along the ice, bouncing off boulders, tumbling and rolling.

I recalled being confused, remembered how hard the ice and boulders felt when I hit them, and then I took another crack on the head and I didn't know anything more until the other musher was yelling at me.

From what I could piece together later, I'm lucky I wasn't killed. I did several miles of Dalzell—the worst part—dragging, and had my dogs not been caught, I could have been almost literally destroyed.

* * *

When I limped into the Rohn River checkpoint, it was dark and I felt (and looked, from what I could see later that day—I was bruised all over) like walking wounded.

I signed in and out, found a place in some trees next to the small log cabin that was the checkpoint, and settled the team in for the night, feeding them, rubbing shoulders and checking feet, heating food for the next leg.

I was doing all these things automatically, working through the pain in my head—a doctor told me later I had probably been concussed—but in truth, the hot worm had come to me. In some part of my mind, it had formed, the thought of quitting, the thought that this wasn't possible for me.

It went in this rational way: I was being brutalized. The dogs were fine, getting better, having a blast— but I was being destroyed.

Why? Why subject myself to such punishment?

Since there was no logical answer for that—why would *anybody* do this?—my mind went to the next step: rationalization.

It wasn't like *really* quitting.

I'd already come farther than most of the rookies who scratched—many did not make it to Rainy Pass, let alone over the damn thing.

And then a flood: I was forty-three, for Christ's sake, I had a family, a chance for success, I had a *life* Down Below—what in the name of god did I think I was *doing* up here?

And I would have quit then. One of the assistant race judges came to look at my dogs with the vet and all I had to do was look at him and say, I scratch.

That easy.

I scratch.

And home to a warm bed and a bath and a hot meal and and and . . .

I looked at Cookie instead.

It was dark, and as I swept my headlamp across her, she stood and looked down the trail.

Just that. We hadn't been in this checkpoint ten minutes. The dogs knew they were to rest and eat; Cookie worked harder than any of the others, should have been more tired, but she stood.

Clean and ready.

Stood to leave and, in that simple act, it was taken from me—any ability to scratch was removed.

She—they would run. It was their race as much as it was mine, more so.

They would run. I didn't have the right to quit.

So I went into the cabin and had somebody tape up my chest with the black electricians tape I used for taping booties on the dogs' feet. My ribs hurt most and the taping helped.

Then I cooked food, filled the coolers with hot meat, rested the dogs until Max stood and made a new bed—three hours—and at dawn I hooked them up to their tugs and left Rohn River for the next segment, stooped and limping with pain.

❉ ❉ ❉

The Burn.

So much of the race was madness that it becomes meaningless to say that the Burn was mad. But it was—or perhaps more than mad, it was beyond all reason. Hardship aside, it didn't make sense.

There was at first a semblance of a trail but within a mile it disappeared because each team sought a better way (there was none). The dogs would run ahead until the sled jammed beneath a fallen burned tree, whereupon I would use my ax to chop through the tree (dog teams do *not* back up), grab the sled, and drag through the rocks and dirt until the sled caught under the next tree (sometimes only a few yards).

For ninety-two miles.

Add to this a sudden drop in temperature to thirty below, just to multiply the difficulty, and—finally—my complete loss of any touch with reality, and the ingredients were there for a first-rate Fellini film.

About midnight I started hallucinating. Sleep deprivation was the clinical cause and I had already experienced some minor brushes with the phenomenon. But they were truly insignificant—shadows that moved quickly away, lights that were almost but not quite there. Small stuff.

In the Burn that all changed—all stops were pulled out and I entered a world of mixed reality and dreams, peopled with the most bizarre souls and creatures so that it's difficult to remember what really happened.

It started simply enough. I was hacking through a tree to loosen the sled when a thin man wearing a corduroy suit jacket, glasses, and a tie stepped up to my right and smiled.

"It's about time somebody showed up to help me," I said. "This shit is getting ridiculous."

And he helped. He did not speak but he helped hold the tree while I chopped and grabbed at the handlebar when the sled blew forward, jumping on at the last second to ride to the next fallen tree.

On the way we passed a woman—quite lovely and completely nude—sitting on a grassy hummock. She beckoned to me to come but I shook my head. "I've got to keep moving," I said. "It's the race . . ."

She nodded and ran up to us, light and lovely on her feet, and jumped on the sled. "I'll ride with you."

The other man was still there and I worried that there would be a mess because he seemed overly interested in her and *I* was interested as well, and getting damn jealous and wondering how I could have some time alone with this beautiful creature and I blinked and they were gone and I was looking out over the dog team at the coast of California just north of Santa Maria. There were surfers working ten-foot curls, men and women both, and I was pleased to see the checker who had told me to watch out for the down part of Rainy wearing a string bikini hanging ten on a short board, and I blinked and there was a herd of wildebeest being chased by wild dogs led by Cookie, and I blinked and there was my wife beckoning for me to release the team and rest.

"Let go," she said. "I'll catch them. Don't worry . . ."

I nearly did, started to let go with one hand, but I blinked and she was gone and the dogs had stopped and Cookie was looking up at a moose.

I blinked. I was learning faster now and while I couldn't make the hallucinations go away, it seemed I could change them by blinking, much like changing television channels.

The moose did not go away.

I blinked again. There were supposed to be no moose in the Burn. I blinked harder.

The moose was still there, looming over Cookie.

I felt a cold not associated with the temperature, a pit of deep fear. There was a sudden picture in my mind of the man holding his dying lead dog, of the moose attack that first night, and I grabbed at something, anything, from the sled to use as a weapon and came up with the ax and ran forward.

It could have all ended there peacefully. The moose could have gone, could have done anything but what it did—it attacked.

In a head-on maneuver it came down the team, kicking as it came, and I went for it with the ax, swinging and hacking, and it hit me and I fell back, fell on the ground, and I scrambled to my feet, raised the ax screaming, "You son of a bitch!"

And it was gone.

I was standing alone, my headlamp sweeping across the gnarled trees and brush. There was no dog team in front of me and I turned in panic, my light flashing back and forth.

No team.

Tracks, I thought. I've got to find tracks. I worked out in a spiral from where I stood, bent over, scanning the light from side to side, studying the ground carefully. Without snow it was hard to tell anything—all scuffs looked alike. On the fourth expanding circle I came across a line in the dirt, one straight line about two feet long where a sled runner had dragged.

Because I was right-handed, and for no other reason, I went right, following the direction the line painted.

Thirty, forty yards I walked in the dark, sweeping the light back and forth. A thousand terrors raced through me. What if they had truly run off? How far would they go? *Where* would they go? How would I catch them?

Another fifty yards, hunched over, peering at the grass and ground, looking for any marks.

When it happened I nearly tripped over them. They were unhooked from their tugs, lying in tight balls, all sound asleep. A fire was going, the dog food pot was next to it, meat was heating.

"What in hell?"

I spoke lowly, but aloud. Cookie awakened and looked up at me but did not rise. I fought to find reason, some sense I could hold.

I had driven the team here without knowing it. I had fed them, unhooked them, settled them in beds, taken off their booties, made a fire, rubbed them down, cooked dog food—all without knowing it.

Then I had taken off alone with an ax in my hand on an imaginary sled, run into an imaginary moose, had an imaginary fight . . .

And nearly lost my team.

I kneeled by the fire, put some more wood on it—I had stocked wood as well before my sojourn—and leaned back against the sled.

Twenty, thirty miles into the Burn. That's all I had come.

"Jesus." I said it aloud, and it was more of a prayer than a curse. Then I used a rope to tie my right wrist to the sled, in case I tried to wander again, and settled back to wait for daylight.

* * *

We moved through the day, rough, but making it, and I had some control over the hallucinations in the daylight.

About noon we came out of a burned stand of scrub spruce along a small ridge that rose to the right, and I was surprised to see a dog team lying at the base of the ridge.

At first I could see no driver and I thought it might be a loose team. But the snowhook had been set and the gear unloaded from the sled, so somebody had stopped deliberately.

"Up here!"

The sound came from above and I looked up the ridge and saw a man lying on his stomach, peering over the top of the ridge. He glanced down at me again.

"Come on up—you've got to see this . . ."

I hesitated. There was not a good base for the hook and being separated from my team the night before was still fresh in my mind.

But the dogs had already started to make beds and settle and would probably stay and in truth I *was* curious. Something had his attention, and when he started to laugh, it was too much to resist.

I set the hook, stomping it into the dirt and grass as best I could, and crawled up the low ridge to lie in the grass next to him and peer over.

We were looking down on a frozen lake—one of the Farewell Lakes located in the Burn. But it wasn't the lake that held his interest. Below and to the right a group of four buffalo were standing on the shore. Two of them were in the grass at the edge and the other two were out on the ice.

Somebody had told me there was a herd of buffalo in the Burn but I hadn't expected to see them along the trail.

"Yes," I told the other musher. "Buffalo. I know. They told us . . ."

"No—watch."

I turned back, thinking frankly that he was around the bend. So it was buffalo—so what? Hell, I'd seen the checker surfing in a string bikini—what the hell was a buffalo?

Then I saw what he meant.

The surface of the lake was bare of snow, as was all the Burn, and the two buffalo out on the ice were having a rough time of it trying to stand.

"What the hell are they doing out there?" I asked.

"Shhh . . . watch now."

So I shut up again and had almost decided to get back to my dogs when one of the buffalo on shore backed away from the lake, up the sloping side of the ridge, pawed the ground a couple of times and ran full bore for the lake.

Just as he hit the edge of the ice his tail went straight in the air, he spread his front feet apart and stiffened his legs and slid away from shore, spinning around in a circle as he flew across the ice.

When he slowed to a stop he bellowed, a kind of "Gwaaa" sound, then began making his torturous way back to the shoreline.

While he was doing this the fourth buffalo came shooting out on the ice, slid farther (also tail-up) than the last, made a louder noise, and started back, slipping and falling.

I couldn't believe it and blinked rapidly several times, thinking I was hallucinating.

"No—it's real," he laughed. "I was passing when I heard the bellow and came up to check it out."

"How long . . . ?"

"I've been here an hour, maybe a little more. They've been doing this all the time. Great, isn't it?"

We lay there for another half-hour watching them play. The object seemed to be who could slide the farthest and each of them tried several times, tail up, happy bellows echoing on the far shore of the lake as they slid across the ice.

"Buffalo Games," he said as we finally backed down the ridge and awakened the dogs. "Buffalo Games in the Burn. Who would have thought it could happen?"

And it wasn't until later, when I finally reached the cabin that marked the end of the bad part of the Burn—not until I was pulling into Nikolai that I realized it made perfect sense. Where else but in the upside-down madness of the Burn could there be Buffalo Games?

McGrath

The Burn fried me mentally and destroyed me physically. Without a snow cushion for the sled the jarring of the ground was brutal—like downhill skiing in bad moguls for thirty-six hours straight. My legs were in agony and I had started to bleed anally from hemorrhoids, which were to get worse and lead me to buy sanitary napkins in a store in McGrath and wear them the rest of the race.

I left the collection of huts that was Nikolai in midday, after sitting on the sled in the sun all morning "resting" the dogs. Out in the wind it had been cold, but with a building in back of the sled to block the wind and the sun heating down it was positively warm—about zero—and I lay back and baked. At the start of the race, day and night were split almost evenly. But daylight was gaining by seventeen minutes each day so we'd picked up over another hour and a half of daylight and I took advantage of every minute of relaxing warmth I could.

As a matter of fact I would have stayed longer except that the race intervened. Against all predictions— my own very definitely included—I was not running last.

Somehow I was running in the high thirties out of seventy teams. I was in no way competitive, and knew it, and in fact I had very serious doubts that I would finish. But I wasn't running last and so while one part of me wanted to lie in the sun and relax, every time a team hooked up and left I would feel the urge to do the same.

At length, when the third team pulled out I said to hell with it and hooked up the tugs and we ran to McGrath.

The run over was a textbook trip. The dogs ran flawlessly. It is all river running, or nearly so, and consequently flat and easy going.

At one point after dark, we entered a section of the river where it wound back and forth so much it was possible to run a mile but move forward only a few hundred yards. I could see the lights of McGrath on the horizon and they seemed so close I could touch them, yet we didn't get there for four more hours, until after dawn.

I was fast becoming a connoisseur of checkpoints. Finger Lake was not so good, seemed disorganized; Rainy Pass Lodge and Rohn River were both better; Nikolai seemed less organized.

I paused after pulling up into town off the river ice. Within moments a checker came out of a building and signed me in and out, pointed out where the food sacks were and where I could rest my team. All in a minute or less. I put the team down to rest and went to get my food from a pile next to a large store.

I was walking back to the team with the sacks, past the front of a cafe building next to the store, when somebody opened the door of the cafe and the smell that came out stopped me dead.

It was so strange—a hunger of such intensity that my mind seemed consumed by it, like being in love.

I had been eating poorly, often not at all. A meat patty here and there, but I had been driven by such excitement that hunger simply hadn't been a factor.

Now it was—absolutely riveting, hunger so vicious that I could think of nothing else. A meal, a sit-down hot meal, became the only thing in my mind. I put down the food sacks and walked into the cafe.

It was a narrow building with a counter and stools down the right side. Still in full arctic gear—parka, wind pants, down pants, mukluks, inner gloves, second gloves, full sheepskin mitts—I sat at one of the stools.

"Would you like something to eat?" A waitress came up to me.

I took a menu from the little rack and opened it. "Anything." I jabbed with a mitted hand. "Here. This."

"Ham and eggs," she said, "and would you like coffee?"

"Barrels of it. Please."

She gave my order to a man in the rear who was cooking and I simply sat, staring at the menu, marveling at all the wonderful things on it.

"You can take your gear off," she said when she brought the coffee. She was smiling. "We have a heater in here."

"What—oh." I nodded. "I just forgot for a minute . . ."

I shucked out of my parka, mittens, and unzipped the sides of my down pants to open them and let the warm air in.

I sipped the coffee, holding the cup in hands almost indescribably filthy. My beard was full of ice as well and I felt it drip as it melted.

There was a brief second of hesitation when the plate came—two eggs, yellow yolks up, a good slab of ham, and a pile of hash browns—so that I could appreciate how wonderful it looked. Then I inhaled it, almost literally. I remember seeing the plate and I remember eating—using a fork or knife—but not individual actions. Everything just seemed to disappear and when it was done the waitress stood in front of me.

"Goodness," she said. "That was quick. Do you want more?"

I looked at her and I must have nodded because she vanished and was back shortly with another plate just like the last: ham, eggs, and hash browns.

And again, I seemed to swallow it whole. And once more she stood in front of me and smiled. "Still hungry?"

I looked at the plate, up at her, and said nothing but she nodded and turned away.

Five times.

I sat there and ate five complete ham and egg breakfasts without a pause, ate them, and when I was done still felt hungry—but stopped in embarrassment. As I stood to pay at the end of the counter, the cook came out of the rear. He was a burly man who could have doubled for the cook in the Beetle Bailey strip. The total bill was horrendous—sixty or seventy dollars (Alaska interior prices had kicked in; every egg, every piece of food in the breakfast had to be flown in by bush plane)—and as I was digging for money he held up a hand.

"Aren't you one of the mushers?"

I nodded.

"Then your money is no good. Have a good run . . ."

And he wouldn't. No matter how I tried he wouldn't take money. I finally left some on the counter for the waitress and went out to the dogs, and many times later on that run I would remember eating those five breakfasts sitting in the cafe in McGrath while my beard ice melted and dripped.

The Interior

The beginning of the battle to cross the interior of Alaska by dog starts when you leave McGrath. The distance to be run to reach the Bering coast is something on the order of seven hundred miles—say, from Minneapolis to New Orleans—and the terrain is so varied and difficult that it is well there has been the Burn and crossing the Alaska Range to prepare one.

At first it does not seem such a very bad thing. After leaving McGrath the trail winds on the river and then comes to a bar where wonderful hosts hand out bag lunches and soft—or hard, if you choose—drinks to take us on our way to the last checkpoint before the interior at the town (nearly so) of Ophir.

We hit Ophir after dark and I put the team down for a couple of hours while I worked on their feet.

They lay, holding up their feet automatically for oint-ment, but did not sleep hard and kept fussing so I hooked them up and headed out in darkness.

Because it was not totally pitch I left my headlamp off, and we hadn't gone far before I felt the sled drag-ging. It kept moving—they could have pulled a Lin-coln by this time—but was dragging funny and I stopped to inspect the runners. As I did so I turned my headlamp on and saw that the runner was coated with a full half-inch of dog crap. And more, with the light on I saw that we were running in a three-foot-wide swath of fresh dog shit. I had not seen this before but it would be this way after many of the remaining checkpoints. The dogs are fed heavily in the check-points and then rested. As they get more professional about running, they understand the checkpoints and what they mean. They know that when they leave the checkpoint they are going to have to pull for some dis-tance and they do not want to carry any extra weight so they "blow" themselves on their way out. Conse-quently, there is a sea of fresh dog crap leaving each checkpoint.

I set the hook and flipped the sled on its back and used a pocket knife to scrape the plastic runner shoes clean. This all took some time and dawn came while I was scraping. When I was finished I flipped the sled upright, pulled the snowhook, and looked out over the team at a completely different world.

It was, somehow, almost a different planet—like suddenly being transported to the moon, or Mars. We were on the face of a shallow but very high hill, the sun coming up to the right rear. Out in front and below us lay a huge plain, stretching off to the horizon and beyond. Here and there at vast intervals there were small stands of low brush, and in the distance I could just make out low hills and rolling ground. Other than the odd bits of brush it was treeless and seemed barren. There was very little snow covering the grass—a constant, driving wind blew the snow away—which added to the alien barrenness.

* * *

Cookie stopped as if to say, "You can't be serious about wanting to cross *that?* . . ."

And in truth I wasn't thinking anything of the kind. A part of me simply didn't understand the enormity of trying to cross the interior of Alaska by dog team. I could be out there a month, I thought, and never seem to have moved. It . . . was . . . endless.

But in another way I was dazzled by it, and hopelessly drawn to it. Race or no race, life or no life— there was nothing that could keep me out of it, out of the interior.

"Pick it up," I said, to nudge her. "Let's go see it . . ."

She jerked once and started them down the incline and out into Alaska.

The part we were going to see was what I had come to think of as the true north—the tundra sweeps, the Barrens. I had read books about it since I was a child, had felt the lure of it, the northern pull of it.

And now I was going to cross it by team.

Within a few miles I was locked into a mystical dance with the sweeps. I had come to love running dogs as much as I loved the dogs themselves; had come to love the harsh beauty of the woods.

But not like this. Something about this, the tundra, the hugeness of it, went inside me and is there still.

I think now that this was my final break with the normal world. Back there somewhere, back in the real world I had a wife and family, a life. But here, now, was everything I needed, everything I was; the sled, food, fifteen good friends—or fourteen friends and Devil, as it happened—all that I had become. I was complete, and part of that completeness was that we, the team and I, were in some way doing what we were meant to do—heading north into the sweeps.

The breakdown of the run across Alaska to get to the Yukon River was simple in its intent—simple and stark.

Leaving Ophir, we were to run 180 miles to the old ghost town of Iditarod, then another hundred or so over to Shageluk, just before getting on the river ice. The first part, the 180-mile run, is the longest run in the race between checkpoints. It requires carrying extra food and booties and gear in case there is a storm, and therein lies the one true problem of the run across the interior. There is enough time elapsed in the run for weather patterns, for whole climates to change.

The dogs move ten miles an hour (or in my case about seven). For short bursts they can go faster, but not for long. Ten miles an hour for four, five hours, then rest for four or five, then again, and again, around the clock. Climbing slows them drastically, as does deep snow—down to two, three miles an hour. Distance becomes meaningless measured in miles because the speed is so variable. A little thing like dog crap frozen to the runners and not discovered will cut speed by thirty percent. As the time shifts (it really proves to be devastatingly relative in the race) it always seems to slow forward progress.

When we started, the weather was wonderfully clear. The sun rose to our right rear and splashed a new gold light across the barren ground and made it glow. The dogs seemed to like the light and picked up the speed a bit and I thought—foolishly baiting the gods—hell, this won't be so bad.

The sky was clear except for two small wisps of clouds on the far horizon that I chose to ignore and we slid effortlessly on the snow and patchy grass down the long slope.

Until almost exactly midday everything went well.

The two clouds seemed to grow. I noted that as afternoon came. They stretched and smeared themselves across the horizon and then up in the sky. And the wind picked up a bit, but only a little, and I thought about getting ready for fighting wind but decided there would be plenty of time later.

There wasn't.

We dipped into a depression as we moved around a shallow hill on the right and as we came out into the open the wind tore my head off.

It literally worked inside my parka hood and blew it open and back off my face. With the wind came flowing snow, driving needles of ice taken from the ground and turned into projectiles digging into exposed skin.

I was nearly knocked off the sled by the force of it and just before Cookie disappeared behind a wall of blowing snow I could see her blown to the side so hard she had to crouch and dig with her claws to hold position.

I—we—paused. Usually when the wind hits that way it is in a gust and a moment's wait will give relief.

Not this time. It started hard and it just grew worse. I couldn't see anything, had no idea where to go. The wind had come from our left front and I thought we could steer with it, keeping it on my left cheek, until we came to shelter. But it was not to be. The dogs ran with the wind. Cookie tried to hold them and keep a true course, but they were too much for her and I felt them swinging around until the wind was at my rear, where it would be easier running.

"No, damnit—come around!"

But they would not. And worse, I couldn't hold them. The brakes wouldn't grab in the frozen ground and aside from the stubby frozen tundra grass there was nothing to hold the snowhook.

They just kept going. And because we were now moving with the wind it became easier to move and they increased speed to a full lope. I couldn't see any of the dogs, couldn't tell where we were going and they were now running wide open. I was reminded briefly of the military cliché: "Don't know where we are or where we're going but we're making really good time."

But in truth it was a patent recipe for disaster. I could lose the team or they could pile up and get injured. I grabbed the catch rope and tied the sled to my wrist so I could grab at it as a last chance if I fell off (I did this on advice of another musher who spoke to me after he'd finished the Burn; he had lost his team there and had to walk—as he put it—"across north, and I do mean *North* America").

Then I slammed harder on the brake, rode it with both feet, and kept hollering, "Whoa—whoa, damnit."

But it didn't help. They kept moving, running faster and faster. I couldn't see anything by this time—barely to the other end of the sled, none of the dogs—and could do little but hang on and wait for the wreck.

It did not come. The team held the high rate of speed for half an hour or so, then began to slow and, finally, as I felt the sled come to a level area, Cookie stopped them.

When they stopped I jumped on the hook to try to set it in the grass, then tried to turn and was blown completely off my feet. The only reason I wasn't blown away from the team was the catch rope around my wrist. I tried to swear but the words were torn away by the wind. Seventy, eighty miles an hour, blowing clouds of snow horizontally into and past me—it was a staggering, killing wind.

I knew it was impossible to try and turn the team and run back, impossible to do anything but hunker down and survive.

I crawled hand over hand up the gangline, found each dog already curled into a weather-proof ball, and made my way back to the sled.

It took me only moments to get back to the sled, unzip the sled bag, unroll my sleeping bag inside the sled bag and crawl in. I zipped the sled bag up over my head, bundled up in the sleeping bag, and settled in. There was absolutely nothing else I could do. The weather had taken over.

Outside the wind grew in strength until it shrieked. But the sled bag was tight and the sleeping bag warm—though the temperature was dropping rapidly—and I was comfortable.

My eyes closed, opened, closed again, and I must have slept, although it may have been closer to passing out.

* * *

I do not know how long I slept. It was late afternoon when I had crawled into the sled bag. I awakened once and unzipped the bag enough to look out and see that it was dark and the wind was still howling.

The next time I opened my eyes it was silent, absolutely quiet. I heard a strange rasping and realized it was the sound of my breathing inside the confines of the bag, but other than that nothing.

I lay for some time, reluctant to break the warm comfort of the bag. And the truth is I'd probably be there still except that nature called.

I unzipped the bag over my head. It felt strangely heavy and as soon as I unzipped it, a large pile of snow fell in on me, finishing the waking-up process, and I stood to a bright, cold world.

We had moved into a shallow depression, a saucer-shaped bowl perhaps a hundred yards across. The bowl was completely filled with snow, blown level with drift-ing clouds of it. I was the only thing standing, or show-ing. The dogs were covered and totally gone. Except for little puffs of steam released up through melted exit holes over each dog's nose where their breath came out, there was no sign of the team, the sled, nothing.

I had to urinate fiercely and I stood to the side of the sled—walking in waist-deep snow—to take care of it. I was not five feet from my sled and fumbling through layers of clothing when suddenly, right where I was going to piss, the snow began moving and a man's head appeared.

"Jesus, it's bright out here, isn't it?"

"Where did you come from?"

He stood and shook the snow off. "Hell, I don't know. We were moving pretty well until the shit hit the fan. Then I couldn't hold them and we wound up here. Must have followed your trail in . . ."

"We? You mean you and the dogs?"

"God, no—we were convoying across the middle. Must have been six, seven teams in our group."

"Where are they?"

He looked around the small basin. "Here."

And they were. Cookie had heard me talking and I saw her head peep out of the snow and swivel around, looking at the day. Devil popped up next, then Max—finally rested enough—and Devil growled at Max and the noise caught other ears and in a second the whole basin exploded in dogs and people standing and shaking off snow, fighting, snarling, pissing, and stretching. Eleven full teams, close to two hundred dogs and ten people had followed us into the small bowl and dug in to ride the windstorm out and I hadn't heard a sound.

But more. We all fed dogs and cooked hot coffee on dog food cookers and stopped to have a cup and visit (we were, by this time, several hundred miles behind the teams leading in the race) and in the ensuing bullshit session one of the men stopped us all.

"Did you hear my shots?"

"What shots?" another man asked.

"When I got in I fired three times, paused, then three more to signal the teams in back of me . . ."

"With what, a cap gun?"

"Hell no, my .44 mag. Six rounds."

He had been less than twenty feet from me—albeit downwind—and fired six times with a .44 magnum, an absolutely deafening handgun, and we hadn't heard it.

We did not believe him and would not except that he took the handgun out of his sled and showed us the empty shell casings as he reloaded. The wind had carried the sound away.

We finished the last of the coffee and some honest to god doughnuts that one man had somehow brought intact from Ophir (half a delicious, wonderful doughnut for each; dipped in hot coffee, it was almost god given).

Still nobody seemed to want to leave and the hesitation was broken at last by one man who voiced all our fears.

"If that fucking wind comes up again, I don't want to be alone. Let's convoy over to Iditarod . . ."

And we all agreed instantly, though none had dared say it. It was the same man who had brought the doughnuts, and I thought how nice he seemed as we lined our teams out and headed back for the trail. To share the doughnuts that way and help us all get going, headed in the right direction. Just an all-around nice person, and I felt grateful that he was with us.

I would never have guessed that I would see him commit murder not ten hours later.

Don's Cabin

Roughly halfway across the long run to the Iditarod checkpoint there is a small shack. It is not an official stop, just a run-down old trappers' hut that the bears tear apart every summer looking for food. But in an early race, a musher named Don, who was from New York, got into a storm like the one we had experienced. Don had been near death when he came on the old cabin and the shelter had saved him. Ever since then he sets the shack up with food, has a crew go in before the race and repair bear damage, and almost every musher stops there to have a cup of coffee and rest his dogs.

We arrived there in a train, the eleven teams spread back over a mile. Most elected to go on to the checkpoint at Iditarod. But the doughnut musher said he was going to stop and work on his team. I had noticed that several of my dogs had runny stools, which can come from stress, overeating, or a virus, and thinking they were stressed (I was wrong—they were eating like wolves and I had been ignorantly feeding them too much), I hung back as well, which was why I was in a position to see the crime.

The bond that occurs between driver and dogs is truly wonderful. It is more than love, becomes something close to what a mother must feel for her child with the added fact that the bond with sled dogs in particular is almost intensely symbiotic. The person gives care—warm meat broth, shoulder rubs, foot ointment and booties, vaccinations, nursing, and of fundamental and vital importance, protection. The dogs give everything they are or can be. In the case of lead dogs and the decisions they must make, their choices can literally mean life or death for the team and driver, often when the driver can't see what is happening.

Dogs rarely violate this relationship—virtually never. Devil might bite me, might kill other dogs, but by god, he pulled and would die pulling and that was a kind of love. I have watched them work, always in awe—and not a little love—and sometimes what they are, out ahead of me, the curve from me up through the sled and gangline into the dogs, all of us moving for some new horizon, sometimes it becomes more, becomes spiritual, religious.

While the dogs rarely violate this relationship, man—or some men—seem to have worked hard at ruining it. Arctic and Antarctic exploration is a terrible, grim page in the history of dogs and sleds and man. Historically, the way of running those expeditions was to start with many dogs and kill them and eat them (and feed them to other dogs) as the expedition moved on. In Antarctica there are still places named after this shame . . . like Butcher Plateau . . . named for where they stopped to kill dogs.

And in truth, the original Iditarod trail—the dog freight trail across Alaska to supply miners and prospectors—was steeped in inhumanity. It is said that at the height of the Klondike gold rush, it was impossible to find a dog in Seattle. Any dog seen was stolen and taken up to Alaska to pull freight—either sleds or carts. They were worked to death and their bones still lie along the trails.

Dogs can cause frustration, it is true. Especially if the human does not know them, how they react. If a dog becomes ill—they catch colds, get headaches, toothaches—they will back off on their pulling, and to the uninformed, it may seem like they're slacking off. A tiny cut, almost microscopic in size, between their toes will make them not push as hard with that foot, and that may be interpreted as an apparent backing off, which is not really the case. They vary as much as people, and allowances must be made for individual personalities, small injuries, illness, boredom, sex (if a female goes into heat, the cure is to rub Vick's on her reproductive organ to hide the smell with menthol, which works fine until the dogs know what it means and then you can't open a jar of Vick's without getting jumped).

If a person cannot deal with all these things, cannot deal with dogs as individuals and make those necessary adjustments in his or her makeup, then they should not be running dogs. It is as simple as that.

Unfortunately, there are people out there running races with dogs who shouldn't have dogs. Not many, because the process weeds them out. Sooner or later, if they are pushed too hard either mentally or physically, sooner or later the dogs themselves will stop. They will lose all love and respect for the driver and they will lie down and quit.

But it takes a lot. Dogs will sometimes die before they lose the love, will love while they're being destroyed.

And that is what happened with the doughnut man's dogs.

When my team was ready, I looked over at him. We were the last two teams to leave and I assumed we would run together and I think he tried.

But his team wouldn't rise.

I had heard of this, and even seen it in a limited way when I had been an asshole during a day of training and told Cookie to go in a direction she knew was wrong. We had gone off an embankment into a gully because of my error and the whole team became so angry with me they laid down and wouldn't get up until *they* decided it was time to go. But it had been brief and I had understood the message and taken it to heart and listened to them when they told me something from that time on.

This was different. I did not know this man, had never seen him run dogs, but clearly there was something terribly wrong with his team and he had done something bad with them. They seemed completely down, beaten, driven in some way into the ground. They tried to move away from him and when held in place by the gangline and tugs they instead tried to hide beneath each other—anything to avoid the man who was now leaning over them with his fist raised, screaming.

He had his back to me so I could not see his face but his body was rigid, stiff with anger. He swung at one of the dogs nearest him with his hand and the dog ducked away so that he missed. He aimed for another blow at a different dog and this one, too, dodged and avoided the strike. Then he changed and reached for the dogs, tried to pull them, jerk them to their feet, working up the team and back down again, his rage growing so that his voice was incoherent, bubbling and seething with it. But they would not rise. He would snatch them to their feet but they would immediately crumple back into the snow.

He faced me now, had worked around the team so that he was facing in my direction, but I do not think that he could see me in his fury. I was quite close— twenty, thirty feet—close enough to see that his eyes were red with blood and anger and he could not see past it, past the dogs in front of him.

Then he did it. With great deliberation he selected one of the dogs near his feet, a small brown dog with a white ruff of fur around its neck and a thick, dense coat, and he kicked it.

He did not kick it to get it up. He was wearing bunny boots—large, heavy, rigidly insulated boots that weigh three or four pounds each, boots that easily become weapons. He kicked with one of these boots and he did not kick simply to make the dog rise and run.

"You son of a bitch," he hissed, "you dirty son of a bitch, I'll teach you not to duck . . ."

And all the time he was kicking the dog. Not with the imprecision of anger, the kicks, not kicks to match his rage but aimed, clinical, vicious kicks. Kicks meant to hurt, to hurt deeply, to cause serious injury. Kicks meant to kill.

He kicked the dog in the head and it screamed in pain and again in the head and then carefully, aimed carefully and with great force, in the side just to the rear of the rib cage. The dog's screams had gone on all this time but with the last kick—the blow must have almost literally exploded the dog's liver—the dog fell back and grew still and it was over, in seconds it was over and he looked up at me, directly at me, and I saw things I had never seen, never want to see again. I saw hate, self-hate, hate and rage and such savagery that I drew back and suddenly understood Nazis and rabies and rape and pillage and My Lai and the death camps and all the horrors that men have done to other men and to themselves in hate, pure hate, and I thought I should kill him.

Now. I should kill the son of a bitch. He has murdered and is worthless, is shit and I should just kill him and I think my hand actually moved toward the ax in my sled and it was very lucky I did not have a gun or I honestly think I might have shot him.

To do that, I thought—to be able to do that to a friend, a close friend who has pulled you halfway across Alaska and wants only to love and be loved and to pull and see the next hill and is now gone. Killed. Murdered. To savage a dog that way, a friend—he could do anything.

The screams of the dog and the man's brutality had affected my team as well and they had pulled to the side in fear and I think loathing—certainly I felt that—and I pulled the hook and left then. It was over and nothing would come of staying there other than to fight or argue and that wouldn't help. All that would help now was to tell the officials at the next checkpoint so that he would be out of the race and perhaps out of dogs.

The rules are strict and enforced and very plain: if you kill a dog during the race for any reason you are instantly disqualified and barred for life from racing in the Iditarod (and virtually all other races in North America when word gets around). I was determined to stop this man and would tell what I saw in the next checkpoint. (I did so and he claimed that the dog had attacked him and he'd kicked in self-defense—a plain lie—and it was his word against mine, or would have been, except that one of the other mushers had stopped his team to adjust something on his sled just over a small rise and had seen the whole thing and corroborated my story. The killer was duly disqualified and barred and I think is still out of dogs.)

The incident tainted the run for me for a time—as it would for anybody who witnesses anything so inhumane. Dog care is very strictly controlled in the race, as it should be, and there are physical examinations and drug checks and vet checks at the checkpoints to make absolutely certain that no single dog is being mistreated. Because of this and the intense dedication and love the vast majority of mushers have for their dogs there are far fewer dogs injured or mistreated than horses or greyhounds at a racetrack or rodeo stock. Mistreatment is almost unheard of in the race, so rare that when it does happen it stands out and jolts all the more for its infrequency, and I ran in stunned shock for miles thinking of the mad hate of the man and indeed the feeling did not leave me until I at last reached the ghost town of Iditarod and told an official what I had seen.

Once a booming gold-mining town with thousands of people, Iditarod is now nothing but a building half caved in. The word means "a distant place" in Ingalik and other than giving the race its name there was little to note and I left as soon as I had reported, picked up my food, and signed in and out.

Shageluk

Just before starting the run up the Yukon River—which has been touted as the worst, the hardest part of the race—we came to the small village of Shageluk, a checkpoint located in some hills and just a short distance from the river.

We crossed the hundred miles from Iditarod to Shageluk in absolutely splendid weather—sun, a running moon at night, no clouds, no wind (after the initial onslaught before Don's cabin). At one point I saw a herd of caribou that must have numbered three or four hundred and we ran through them so close it seemed I could touch them. They did not unduly fear us, and that seemed strange since a pack of six wolves working the outside edges of the herd scared the hell out of them and caused them to run in panic. I thought they would fear the dogs—especially Devil, who tried several times to free himself from the gangline and harness and drag one down for a snack—but they simply watched in curiosity unless we headed right for them. And then they would just move a few steps to let us pass.

Not long after the caribou, in the middle of a bright afternoon, I was rummaging around in my sled bag while the dogs kept running. At Iditarod one of the other mushers had given me a Butterfinger candy bar and I had saved it carefully for later. Somehow it had fallen out of a small pack I kept on top of the load and settled down between the cracks into the other gear. I was determined and dove in, reaching to the bottom and finally finding it and was just getting ready to rise when the dogs stopped and I barely hit the brake in time to keep from running over the wheel dogs.

In front of me was a sled and team, the team standing, the snowhook set, everything in order, the dogs held properly in place.

And no person.

We were in the middle of a vast plain, flat and treeless, undulating shallow rolls of short, scruffy tundra grass sticking up through an almost dust of snow, and I could see for miles, and there wasn't a person in sight.

I thought I was hallucinating but the dogs were smelling the other dogs and Devil was getting ready to fight and it was broad daylight. Most of the hallucinations occurred between midnight and dawn, very little of it in the afternoon, and when Devil tried to eat one of the other dogs it all proved real. I dragged my team away bodily, set my hook in the grass/snow, and studied the situation.

There was a team here.

There was no person here.

Why would a person run off? Wolves scared him, I thought, or he was crazy and did as I did the night I fought the imaginary moose. Or he was whisked away by spirits . . .

My mind ran wild and I had just decided I would start making circle search patterns when a small movement caught my eye. A quarter of a mile off to the side, in a shallow depression, there was a waist-high bush. It did not have leaves of course and was nearly invisible at that distance, and I wouldn't have seen it at all except that a small figure stood up in back of the bush and started walking toward me.

It was the driver of the team and the figure had come considerably closer before I recognized it as one of the women mushers.

"Are you all right?" I asked, when she was close enough to hear me.

She smiled and nodded. "Had to go to the bathroom—that was the only cover. I didn't want to make the team work extra so I stopped them and walked over . . ."

I looked at the bush. A good quarter of a mile. And not another living soul for a hundred miles.

She read my thoughts. "I've always liked my privacy."

I nodded.

"You know, when I go."

"I understand." And I pulled the hook and left and I think it still might be the record for bathroom privacy.

* * *

When I arrived at Shageluk a small child came running out of a log council building and handed me a large paper bowl with a spoon stuck in it.

"Chili," the little boy said. "Moose chili. For you."

I was still standing on the sled, holding it with the brake, but it was steaming hot and looked delicious and I couldn't wait so I ate it standing there while the boy watched, smiling. I had no more than finished the last spoonful than he grabbed the bowl, ran into the council building, and came out with another full bowl.

Which I ate.

And another.

At length I had to stop him. He just kept bringing them to me and I think I would still be eating them had I not ended it by rubbing my stomach and smiling. "I'm full. It was great. Thank you very much. It was a very nice thing to do—I was starving."

He looked at me and shrugged. "It's all right. That's why we have the pot of moose chili. Just for the dog drivers. But you ate more than any of the others . . ."

"I haven't had hot food since McGrath," I said. "And that was . . ." I couldn't remember time any longer. It simply didn't register. "That was before the run to Don's cabin and the storm and the dead dog and Iditarod . . ." I trailed off.

"My father says you're crazy."

"Me?"

"All of you. The dog drivers. He says you're all crazy. Are you crazy?"

I thought about the old saw that if you think you're insane then you're not insane; truly insane people don't know they're insane. But by this time I frankly knew that I was insane—nobody sane would do this, any of this. "Yes. I'm crazy."

He smiled. "I am nine. I already have four dogs. When I get to be eighteen I am going to go crazy, too, and run this goddamn race."

He ran off then with the bowl. Another team was coming and I saw him come out a moment later with the same bowl—it had a floral design I had smudged with my dirty hands—full of chili that he handed to the driver who ate gratefully, and I moved away to rest my team and prepare for the run up the river.

The Yukon

Two hundred miles straight north up the middle of the Yukon River; three days and two nights. You have to run in the middle exposed to the wind because the snow is too deep on the sides and in places it is half a mile and more wide so the wind gets a really good sweep at you. The problem is the Yukon River Valley is where all the cold air seems to drop in Alaska and it is frequently fifty, sixty below—not wind chill but actual temperature. Cold enough to "piss and lean on it," as they say in the north; cold enough to spit and have it bounce.

Every year they talk about bypassing the Yukon because it is so hard, but every year they run it because it provides a flat highway through hilly and mountainous terrain.

It is, in a word, brutal.

It does not shock, like Happy Canyon or Dalzell Gorge, does not have the slamming and jarring intensity of the Burn, does not awe like the sweeps of the interior.

It's just awful. The river and wind—according to one New York musher who was running the race—is "right in your goddamn face asshole bad."

There is no relief, no way out, no hope . . .

We came down a small stream and onto the river early in the morning after a quick run over from Shageluk just before dawn (and after three more bowls of the delicious moose chili, which had prompted gas so bad that the dogs actually stopped to see what had happened when I farted).

Cookie had loved running down the streambed. It whipped back and forth and she "cracked the whip" on the sled and was having a hell of a good time when we suddenly came out onto the river ice.

Wide, flat, virtually bare ice. There was a scratch-track from a sled before me heading out into the middle and to the right and Cookie started out, then hesitated, glanced back at me with a quizzical look, her ears cocked.

"Yeah. That's it, pick it up . . ."

At first (memories of Rainy Pass) it did not seem so bad. It was daylight, the sun was out, it was perhaps twenty below—a wonderful temperature for running dogs, one they love—and we actually picked up speed as the dogs settled into running on the ice. They slipped a bit initially but quickly found their footing and a method of running that grabbed and we started to really cover the miles. I thought we might be doing over ten miles an hour and calculated that at that rate, including a rest period, we might finish the river in a day and a half instead of the three days we were told it would take in the pre-race briefing. I couldn't then understand what would take three days about running two hundred miles on a flat river. I remember actually thinking, this is a cakewalk.

But again, time was meaningless. All that counted was distance multiplied by difficulty. And cold.

Cold stops.

True cold, deep cold even without wind, intense cold becomes a barrier as solid as brick. And while I had taken thirty, even forty below and some wind, and had even become something close to cocksure about my ability to handle winter, I had absolutely no goddamn idea what was about to hit me. The Yukon River defines that which is cold.

We hung to the middle of the river with the sun warming our backs, the dogs moving easily forward, the sled runners hiss-scritching on the ice and the scenery—as with most of Alaska—stunning.

In mid-afternoon there was a hint, although I didn't quite put it together. We rounded a bend in the river and caught some wind—not a lot, but enough to slow the sled and make the team lug a bit—and at the same time we moved into a shady part, where the sun was blocked by a mountain and the temperature dropped.

It didn't ease down. It dropped like a shot and I felt a sudden, mean chill hit my face.

"Jesus . . ." I had been riding with my parka hood down, although I was wearing a warm hat, and I pulled it up and turned to face off the wind. It felt like my nose was frozen. In less than five seconds.

But then the sled moved back into the warmth of the sun and the river widened to let the wind dissipate and it was gone. Just a kiss of cold but had I been more astute I would have thought what it meant about the coming night. (Although, as the English musher asked me later when we were talking about the run up the river, "What the fuck would you have done— stopped?")

Perhaps there is some bliss in ignorance. As it happened I didn't worry all day and enjoyed the scenery and sunshine and did not begin to sense the menace until the sun went below the mountains on the left.

It was not yet dark—and many hours away from the coldest part of the night, the hours just before dawn—but when the sun slipped below the ridge of the mountains it felt like a hammer blow.

I was not yet alarmed. I had been cold before. I had, after all, run well over half the Iditarod by this time—had done some winter survival of my own.

So it was cold, I thought. So what? I had clothes in my sled bag I hadn't worn yet. Heavier pants, pullover anoraks, masks, sheepskin mitts. It was simply time to bring them out.

I halted the team and snacked them and pulled the extra clothing out of my sled bag. I had to take my parka off to put them on and the cold got a really good shot at me when I did so. I broke records getting redressed and it was then that nudges of what was to come started to hit me. The cold seemed more intense, had more of a cutting edge than I had experienced before.

Still, the full force hadn't come yet and the extra clothing helped, and I went back to work, checking the dogs, feeding them, putting booties on some that needed them, running, watching the tugs. The business of running dogs.

I put my headlamp on, although it wasn't quite dark enough for it yet, and settled in for what I assumed would be a standard night run.

Then it became dark.

And the bottom dropped out.

Cold came at me from everywhere. Any seam, any crack, any opening and I could feel jets of it, needles of it, deadly cutting edges of ice, worse than ice, absolute *cold* coming in.

It was, simply, not believable.

Within an hour I was in trouble. I had on every bit of clothing in my arsenal of cold-weather gear and it wasn't working. I could feel it penetrating me, entering my shoulders, through the mask on my face, inside my parka, under and around and through to cut and chill and bring death.

God, I thought, *god in heaven . . .*

It must have been sixty below. Coupled with a wind that now came up, and the fact that we were moving against the wind at something close to ten miles an hour, and what had been alarming now became dangerous, lethal.

I worried about the dogs and stopped several times to check them for frostbite or any signs of injury but there were no indications. They seemed happy and not to mind the cold and wind and I moved back to the sled and because of checking them I found salvation.

On one of the stops I had set the snowhook in a crack in the ice. It was precarious at best and they could easily jerk it loose and leave me so I hurried when I checked them, jogged up to the front end and back.

And when I arrived back at the sled and pulled the hook, my body felt slightly warmer for the hurried movement.

I started to run then. Not constantly, but I would hang on to the handlebar and run a hundred paces, then ride for a time until I felt the cold penetrate before getting back off the runners to run again.

All night. It was still bad. My cheeks became frost-bitten and my fingers and toes went early but they did not truly freeze and I made the night and even the worst part just before light until the sun—and I understand worshipping the sun now—came back up to give relief and life for another day.

I do not know how cold it became that night, not in degrees, not in the clinical, petty measurements that humans have come to use.

I know that it was so cold the wooden matches struck on the abrasive side of the box would not light no matter how fast or hard they were struck.

I know that it was so cold the batteries on my head-lamp stopped functioning and I ran through the night in the dark—and the batteries were *inside* my clothing.

I know that it was so cold all the plastic packages of ointment and medicine for the dogs' feet, hanging from a cord around my neck and worn inside all the clothing next to my long underwear, the ointment froze absolutely solid.

Cold. So cold that when the sun came up and I felt the warmth on my clothing I wanted to cry and pray at the same time and when, after a second vicious night, I finally arrived at the village of Kaltag, where the trail leaves the Yukon River and heads a hundred miles out to the Bering Sea, I was as grateful as I was when I got out of the army or saw my son born—soul grateful.

Unalakleet

Night and day. The differ-
ence between the interior and the coast was that striking. Somehow the run across and the drive north up
the Yukon, though it had happened in the day as well
as the night, somehow it seemed to be all darkness,
cold and darkness.

The Bering coast was all light and sun and soft
weather.

I left Kaltag and the hated Yukon River just after
dark. I had wanted to rest there and recover from the
damage—mental and some physical—done to me (not
the dogs, they were fine) by the run up the river and
the deep cold, but I ran into one of the problems of the
race that is not openly discussed. To wit: alcohol.

Some of the villages have problems with alcohol, or
more correctly, some of the people in some of the

villages have problems with alcohol. It is of course not limited to the native villages—people across the whole of society have problems with alcohol—but that night in Kaltag I seemed to run into an inordinate number of drunk people.

One woman offered her favors, others wanted to pet the dogs, dance, laugh—party in general—and the upshot was that it would have been impossible for the dogs to get any rest, so I grabbed my food bags, signed in and out, and left while it was still dark.

I knew nothing of the terrain that was coming at me—only that over a ninety-mile stretch we would "drop" to the coast.

Through the dark we ran and I kept waiting for the "drop," shades of Rainy Pass still in my mind, but an abrupt drop never happened. After thirty or so miles of either level or slightly downgrade running, the dogs having a wonderful time and the memory of the Yukon fast leaving me as we moved away from the stone cold, we came around a corner to find a campfire.

It was going well, had melted down through the snow to the ground, and there was a bed of spruce boughs (we were moving through a canyon and there were trees again for a brief time) but absolutely no sign of life. There wasn't a dog team, nor a driver, nor any indication that there had ever been one—although there were fresh snowmachine tracks. I pulled off the trail and tied the dogs and sled to a tree, unhooked their tugs, and settled. We were due to stop anyway to snack and make up for the rest we didn't take in Kaltag, and the fire looked very inviting.

It didn't make sense but I thought that someone must have stopped here and left the fire going and that perhaps wind had blown the tracks and signs away, or covered them.

I broke out my coolers and dog food cooker and put more wood on the fire from a fresh-cut and ample pile near the bed and started cooking dog food and opening my clothing to let the fire warm me more personally. I hadn't been doing this for ten minutes when a team came barreling around a corner and the musher slammed on the brake in a shower of snow and stopped next to me.

He looked at me without speaking.

"Hello," I said. "You looking for a place to stop and rest?" I gestured. "I found a nice fire."

"I . . . uhh . . ." He seemed ill at ease, which didn't make any sense. "Yeah. I'm due for a break . . ."

He pulled his team off on the opposite side of the trail, unhooked tugs, and brought his food and cooker over to the fire.

"Nice bed," he said.

"Yeah. It was here, too. Sorry there aren't two of them."

"I'll cut some branches and make another one . . ."

There was still some tension I couldn't understand but I thought hell, it's the race, he probably thinks he's hallucinating or something, and I stopped thinking about it.

Another five or ten minutes passed and I heard the distinctive two-cycle whine of a snowmachine and within moments a machine came screaming down the trail.

This was not something unusual. One of the great hazards of the race was snowmachines, especially being driven by drunks. Along with planes they are the main form of transportation in the winter in Alaska, and along the Yukon River—a highway across the middle—they come screaming by at sixty, seventy, eighty miles an hour. During the day it can be bad enough, especially if it's off the river and they come around a corner blind and hit the team. But at night it's worse. They move at speeds that make it impossible for the driver to react if he sees something in his headlights, and there are many accidents. Teams are hit, dogs have been killed, people injured and some killed. I had developed a healthy respect—fear—for the damn things and would stop and pull my team off the trail when I heard one coming, waving my headlamp back and forth to warn them.

But this one didn't go by. ,

It whipped around the corner and pulled off and stopped by the fire and the driver was off the machine holding an insulated parcel before he realized there were two of us there.

It stopped him. "Oh . . ." And a look passed between him and the other dog driver and I understood suddenly what was happening. They were friends and the man on the snowmachine was helping. He had made the fire, set up the bed, had it all ready for his friend and then gone for . . .

"What's in the box?" I asked.

"Oh, nothing. I just went to Unalakleet and

bought a pizza." The machine driver shrugged. "You know, for later."

"What kind of pizza?"

"Sausage. Extra cheese."

"And it's still hot?"

He nodded, but held the pizza in its thermos container under his arm protectively.

I looked at my dogs. I had snacked them earlier and they were settling for the rest cycle. To feed them now would disturb them. I would feed them later, after they had rested. I had time. And the situation was clear: there was a violation of the rules here. Nobody is allowed to help. People can't even preheat your water for you in the checkpoints; can't feed your dogs, build your fire. Nobody can help a musher except another musher in the race—and even that has restrictions.

To have somebody run ahead of you on a snowmachine and build fires and make beds and then go out for hot pizza . . .

No. That wasn't allowed. Period.

And I could turn them in and the dog driver would undoubtedly be disqualified.

But we were all well out of the money, were in no way competitive, so what we did wouldn't affect the race.

And there was that pizza.

God, I thought, has brought me a pizza.

"Oh, hell." The other dog driver sighed. "Would you like a piece of pizza?"

I shrugged. "I guess—if it's not imposing."

"No, no problem . . ."

And we all sat around the fire and ate pizza that was only a little cold—he had whizzed over from Unalakleet, about sixty miles, in under an hour on the snowmachine—and talked about dogs and drank Cokes that he had brought to complement the pizza, and all the cares of the Yukon were taken from me.

Just before daylight I hooked up tugs and left them, still camping by the fire, and in fact would not see either of them again until Nome.

* * *

Unalakleet was coastal, and Eskimo, and made up of small government houses and log food caches on stilts (to keep the food away from the dogs) and frames that held canvas tents in summer. It was one of the few places where we were allowed to stay in houses, and the people in the village had signed for mushers, each family taking in a different one. They were wonderfully hospitable and had white bread and beans and sauerkraut and grape jelly—all flown in at great expense for me—and about twenty absolutely delicious caribou (reindeer) steaks (I think I ate them all but saved the grape jelly for the children, who were hovering nearby).

I simply could not get enough food. They didn't make enough food. I was dropping a little over a pound a day and eating everything I could find. I had eaten all the food I sent for myself, all the food the people in the village cooked, and I went to the leftover pile and found reindeer sausage left by other mushers. Everybody ships more than they'll need to each checkpoint in case there are storms and you have to hole up to ride them out. There is an enormous surplus and I found human food left in the pile and ate that. Starting at the Yukon I ate as much as I could as often as I could—even eating sticks of butter straight—and I still lost over a pound a day and was hungry all the time.

Much of the race had become mystical to me. The hallucinations caused part of it, of course, and the god-awesome beauty of the country, but the focus of the spiritual feeling came with the Bering Sea.

I am not sure why, but it transported me. I spent a full night in Unalakleet—eating and fixing broken and worn gear, sewing harnesses and torn clothing, listening to stories, and dozing sitting at the kitchen table in the small government house, looking out the window at the team and waiting for Max to make a new bed.

He did not move so much as a whisker until an hour before daylight. I went out then and hooked tugs, and while I was doing it I wondered for the last time about my other, my old life. It all seemed strange now, as if it belonged to someone else. My life was the team, was taking care of feet, feeding dogs, caring for them, standing to the sled, looking at the horizon.

Cities, wife, son, work—all of it seemed alien now, *was* alien now. It is said that if you can do something new for twenty-one days it will become a habit. I was thirteen days into the race, but many more than twenty-one in training, being with the dogs, and it was an accurate statement—I had changed, re-formed. I had gained knowledge that I didn't understand. I re-flexively knew where the wind would be worst on a hill, knew where to watch for moose, knew in my mind the shoulder rhythms of trotting and running dogs and what it meant when they changed.

I could not stay inside a house. Again and again I went to the wall, the window, and finally an old man who had been sitting at the table with me laughed and said something to the others (people, young and old, seemed to have been circulating through all night) that I didn't get.

"What?" I asked, turning from the window.

"You have become one of them," he said. "A dog. You pace, you look out, you move . . . like a dog."

"I smell like one, too . . ."

He nodded, smiling. "Yes. You do. Only with that other smell there, too, the smell that comes from white places. But that is going away. Tell me now, isn't this better?"

"What?" I had been looking at the dogs again.

"This—this way to live. With the dogs and the sled and the snow. Isn't it better this way than the way you live the other times?"

"Down below?"

He nodded. "All that. How can you live that way? I see it on television and I do not understand how you can live that way. Isn't this better?"

And I nodded. "Yes. It is."

"Good. You finish this goddamn thing and when it is done you get your woman and come back down the coast and live with us. We'll go hunting seals on the ice and your children will get fat and we'll sit and talk."

I smiled.

"You do that now. Come and live with us and leave that other way. It is no good."

It is an invitation that has never left me, is still alive when I think of the coast, the Bering Sea.

❊   ❊   ❊

I hooked up and left just before dawn and ran north along the coast for an hour or so, the trail easy, no wind, and when the sun came up to the east it brought light that seemed to vanish to the west. There was nothing there to catch it, no mountains, no hills, no land—it hit gold on open water (the ice was only frozen out a quarter of a mile or so) and kept going, to Siberia, around the world, beautiful golden light that skittered away forever and I said aloud:

"Look. It's the sea."

And the dogs looked. Not all. I don't think Devil did. You couldn't eat it. But many, and certainly Cookie, and then we jumped a flock of two or three hundred ptarmigan that exploded up like white bombs and the dogs were off and running after them.

I let them run—they were moving in the right direction—until they brought themselves back down to a trot and we moved well through the day, a bright, soft-warm day with the blue water on our left until we slid down a long slope into some willows and came out on the spit of land that led out into Norton Sound where we had to cross seventy-five miles of open sea ice.

There was a small village on the end of the spit— Shaktolik—and we ran the spit in the last of the daylight and hit the village just after dark.

Again we were put up in houses, but here it was different. I was in a room with four other mushers, all of whom had run before, and they were silent and working on their gear, and there was some strain in the room, some unease that didn't make sense.

Finally I asked. "Why is it so quiet?"

"It's the Sound," the man nearest the door said. "Norton Sound. We have to cross the ice. Last year people were nearly killed. They found one man in his sled bag and they figured if they hadn't located him with a plane he'd have been dead in another hour."

As he spoke I happened to be looking out the window. There was a moon showing on the ice, still and beautiful. Tracks from the last sled vanished in the distance. It wasn't cold—maybe twenty below. No wind. It was, in short, absolutely perfect for running dogs.

"I don't get it," I said. "Hell, it's beautiful out there."

But nobody answered. They kept working and the man who had spoken to me stood and shook his parka down over his shoulders and went to the door. He stopped there, not saying anything, his back to the room, then seemed to shrug and put his hand on the door and stepped out. In a moment I heard him hooking tugs and the dogs barking, whining to go, and he left while I watched, skidding off the point away from the house and into the distance on the ice.

I was there four and a half hours, resting dogs, waiting for Max, and the other three men left while I waited, each of them reluctant to go, each pausing at the door, and had you told me then that I would very nearly never see them again I would have thought it absurd.

Norton Sound

Seventy-five miles of open, often moving, splitting, heaving sea ice, salt-water ice, broken with pressure ridges and absolutely no cover of any kind if the wind comes for you.

When I left it was still dark and I could actually see the lights from the next checkpoint—the village of Koyuk—seventy-five miles away across the ice. Could see where I would be in two days until the sun came up and stole the lights.

The Sound was starkly beautiful. There was no wind (I was to find this an almost unheard-of exception), and the sun came off the ice to our right and made the ice and sheath-coating of snow brilliantly white. I squinted and I saw Cookie change modes from using her eyes to see the trail to her nose as the sun blinded her, dropping her head to find a scent, then picking up the pace.

I felt, for lack of a better phrase, very arctic. The run so far had all been mountains and rivers and trees and tundra, but this, this was running dogs on sea ice and I thought of all the explorers, all the people who had used dogs on sea ice to hunt and live, and felt a kinship with them.

We went this way for some time, perhaps two hours, almost three, me with my bemused head stuck firmly up my butt, when things suddenly—within seconds—changed.

In the first instant I saw Cookie alter her pace. She had been running with her left shoulder dropped back a bit, a trot-position that allowed her to reach slightly farther forward with her right front leg. Since she was right-handed it was more comfortable for her to run this way. But now she dropped back to a much slower pace, almost a walk, and her tail shot up to the question-mark position. If she was confident about things it hung straight down and to the rear, and the height it went up was in direct proportion to what she perceived as risk. I was very much in tune with the position of her tail—lived by it—and now it was straight up, the tip curved over in a question mark. At the same time she "got light." I felt my heart freeze. When she went up on her tiptoes and tried to be lighter it meant only one thing—bad ice.

Half a second later I felt the sled move. It was the same movement an earthquake makes—a shudder, then a wave, a movement of the whole world,

a slip of the firmament, a shifting of the base of
life.

I damn near crapped my pants. It had happened so
fast. One moment I had gone all arctic, loving the ice,
the sea off to the left a few miles, and now, without
warning, I was going to die. I had gone through ice
before, had been saved only by luck and Cookie's instant reaction, and I knew how quick it went. You
were, quite suddenly, gone. You couldn't swim with all
the clothes on, couldn't stay up even long enough to
scream; you dropped like a shot.

And here I was over god knew how many feet of
Bering Sea.

Initially there had been no visual indication of the
ice changing. I assumed it was six or eight feet thick—
it had that density. But now I studied it more closely
and saw that it was new ice, very new, with a dusting
of snow blown over it. It wasn't a foot thick, perhaps
only two inches, and it was moving, bending, heaving
with underwater surges.

I grabbed the catch rope and fell back from the sled
on my stomach, my legs open to spread the weight. At
the same time I yelled:

"Gee around!"

It was an old trapline command and wouldn't work
on the race dogs. But Cookie knew it meant to swing
out to the right and bring the team back around to get
out of a tight spot.

They fought her for a bit, tried to go straight, but
she found a crack in the surface and got her nails in
and dragged them around with me skidding in back on
my stomach.

We went that way for a hundred yards or so when I saw Cookie's tail drop and she headed out almost straight east. I felt a bump as my stomach slid off the bad ice and onto the older ice pan.

Investigation later explained what had happened. Sea ice is never static as lake ice usually is. There is great fluidity to it, a flexing and moving, and an enormous cake—twenty miles and more across—had split off and headed out to sea the night before.

New ice had frozen in at once. But it was salt ice, and froze slower than fresh water, and was not nearly as strong.

Two hours earlier and I would have gone through. Perhaps even an hour. People die every year on the ice—some native women have been widowed several times by the time they are twenty-five, husbands lost on sea ice.

And as it happened the man ahead of me was a casualty. I ran around the new spot, adding twenty or so miles to my run as I skirted east and back, and when I got into the checkpoint at Koyuk the checker asked me if I'd seen the man.

"I didn't see anybody out there."

"That's strange—the ham radio operator said he left well ahead of you."

"Yeah—two hours, at least."

"And you didn't see him on the ice?"

I shook my head. "Nothing." And I didn't say it but if he'd been out there I would have seen him.

"How was the ice?"

"Bad . . ." And I told the checker what had happened to me and we decided the man ahead of me had hit it wrong and gone through, team and all. It had happened before—not in the race but in training. Everybody dead. I tried to remember him, how he looked, what he'd said. People would want to know. But all I could come up with was a picture of him swirling down, tangled with his sled and the dogs, dragged down and down into the deep blue of the Sound . . .

I was wrong.

He had been on the piece that caked and split off and went out to sea. The ice was so large that he hadn't known it for a day, just kept running dogs, feeding them, until finally he'd hit water and knew what had happened.

He completely missed one checkpoint. The ice had drifted back to land two days later up near Topkok Head and he'd run off the ice to find himself almost a hundred miles advanced. The rules state that you have to sign in and out of each checkpoint—no excuses—so he was disqualified. But I heard he didn't care. He'd found god out there on the ice alone and was just glad to be able to come back at all and not worried that he didn't get his buckle (you get a brass buckle if you finish the race).

It was dark again when I finally crossed the Sound and came into Koyuk, and I rested the team alongside a building that turned out to be a National Guard Armory. A native man was sitting there in the dark with a headlamp on his head looking down into his lap and making the strangest sounds.

"Aiiiimmmm thuuuu guuuuun . . ."

I went closer and saw that he was reading a Louis Lamour western, using it to learn to read, and I wish

now I had a picture of it. He was sitting on an overturned bucket, leaning against the building, reading
like he was sitting in a living room, and it was forty
below and the wind was starting to pick up on the
Sound, tearing at things, and he was totally immersed
in the western.

Nome

The race is relentless. I had in mind that it was only 150 miles from Koyuk to Nome, and now that I had done the interior and Rainy Pass and the Burn and the goddamn Yukon (it is *still* that to me) and Norton Sound, now that I had done all that I had proven something, and now it would not be so hard, it would be a skate in to Nome.

But the race is relentless; no part of it acknowledges any other part. If it is bad on the Yukon it is not good on the Sound, but can be bad again and still worse yet on the run from Koyuk to Nome.

People have scratched there. There is a mountain to go over, a trail over the middle of the top of Topcok Mountain into the second-to-last official checkpoint at White Mountain, and people have been so bludgeoned they have scratched there. They have scratched on the mountain. They have scratched fifty miles from Nome.

It, the race, does not let up and I was to find that you cannot relax, cannot become weak.

We ran along the edge of the ice to the village of Elim, ran until the sea came crashing into the rocks and broke the ice away and we couldn't run, and then we worked up through the rocks to run on top in the broken terrain, in the nightmare of craggy cliffs and devastated earth that is the coast.

And the wind came then. When it was bad enough to be nearly impossible to run, the wind came and started tearing at us, blowing me down, blowing the dogs away as we wound up Topkok. Right at the top we caught strange currents and I was given the marvel of seeing Cookie suspended in midair, all four feet off the ground, floating on a cushion of high-velocity air as we came over the top of the mountain.

She hung there for two or three seconds and it pissed her off so that when she landed she turned and took a chunk out of Wilson, the point dog in back of her. It was the only time I saw her lose it, and I must have used half a jar of ointment on Wilson's head to stop the bleeding.

Then down the mountain, tumbling and falling, bouncing off moguls and flying through the air. I could not get my feet on the runners and dragged the whole way down to scoot out onto the sea ice again for the run across a small bay to get to White Mountain.

By now the wind was vicious. The ice was completely bare and we weather-vaned so that I was out to the side hanging on the wind while Cookie and the team ran crablike to keep us moving in the right direction.

Nor was it over at the checkpoint. I signed in and out and snacked them but now it was only fifty miles to Nome and I couldn't stop, wouldn't stop.

I don't know if they knew it, sensed it, but they didn't want to rest. (There is a mandatory twelve-hour break at White Mountain now, but then there was not and many people kept going.)

Through the night and into day we ran, fighting the wind, and in late day, afternoon, evening, we came to "the beach." A forty-some-mile-long beach that leads to Nome.

I pulled Cookie left onto the sea ice where there was easier going and we kept moving until at twenty miles we stopped at the Safety checkpoint, the last checkpoint, and it was dark and in the distance, through the gusts of snow, I could see the lights of Nome.

I didn't want to go in. I thought suddenly of the old man who wanted me to come back and hunt seals and live on the coast and I wanted to turn.

But Cookie knew. She saw the lights as well, and she knew and she took over then, picked it up and we ran the edge, still fighting the wind until I heard the siren (they set off a siren for every team that comes in) and we left the sea ice on a long ramp used to launch boats.

Front Street was bare and my plastic runners were about gone so I hung on to the sled and trotted alongside as Cookie pulled the team down the street where a crowd of people were waiting by the finish line.

There were lights and cameras and reporters and my wife and son and the mayor of Nome welcoming me.

"So," a reporter asked. "What have you got to say?"

And I stood in my torn clothing, everything ripped and resewn, a sanitary napkin packed into my bleeding ass, my ability to think gone, my hips and back wrecked from the jolting of the runners; stood in the wreckage of seventeen days, fourteen hours on the trail; stood with spit frozen in my beard and frostbitten cheekbones, two of my toes black; stood in memories of attacking moose and carnivorous wind, the sweeps of the interior out ahead of me; stood in all of that and said with complete belief:

"I'm going to come back and win this son of a bitch . . ."

An End

He was wearing an off-white smock covered with small pictures of Disney animals. Mickey Mouse, Donald Duck, Huey-Dewey-Louie, Scrooge McDuck.

The doctor.

He'd been seeing a child, or children, just before he came into my cubicle and he had the same smile he would use for children. A small smile. A small sad smile.

The tests were done. Treadmill, cardiogram, angiogram, and he held the folder in his hand, the manila folder. Little Disney animals and the manila folder. I was in bed with my groin taped with an elastic bandage to compress the hole in my leg artery where the probe went in.

"Well, the tests are positive." The smile left, came back but smaller. He looked into my eyes. Directly into them. It was a course they take in medical school: Bedside Manner 101. Always make eye contact with the patient. Especially if the news is bad. Very bad. "Of course that's negative. I mean the test is positive but that's a negative thing to find out. You have coronary heart disease."

But.

That was the first word. First thought. Just that. But.

But I'm training for my third Iditarod.

But my son hasn't graduated from college yet.

But I've just become successful and started dieting and have a new idea for a book and found a measure of spiritual grace and learned some of the rhythms, the pulses of words, and haven't made love to Cher yet and haven't learned how to release, release the bowstring . . .

But.

Cold chill. At the base of the spine.

It became important to tell him how it happened, very important, singularly important. "I was in the Boston airport and had gone there on business, and I felt it then and went down on one knee, I think it was the left one . . ." I trailed off. Small cold place there and I wanted to go to the bathroom or turn around and go back and not eat all those pork chops and the fear grew, moved up my back, and turned into army fear and then bar-in-Juarez-when-the-man-pulls-the-knife fear and it settled in my stomach.

But.

Have to keep up the facade. I wanted to scream, to rip and growl and tear, but I kept my voice cool—oh shit, yes, cool—James Bond. "Is there a time?"

He misunderstood and shook his head and I felt the fear grow, suddenly shot into my chest. *Fuck,* I thought. *Not* but *anymore but* fuck. *I'm going to die.* I smell it then—death. Smell-taste it. Copper, just like they say in all the books—a copper-blue taste and my body tightened and I felt like I had to shit. Right then. My forehead was sweating and I looked at the clock on the wall. Big clock. Like they used to have in schools. Stuck on the wall of the small room.

The hand had not moved. No time had passed since he told me. No time. But everything had slowed, almost to a crawl. The nurse was smiling as well but it was pity and I locked onto it for a moment. The sad pity of it all. She knew. The nurse knew. The Madonna knew.

The doctor realized his mistake and touched my arm. "No . . . no. Not like that. You have a nearly blocked artery on your heart. There are many forms of treatment available, up to and including bypass surgery. You're not dead yet . . ."

I took a breath, let it out. I remembered each part of that breath. In, hold, out.

"Because you've been so active with the dogs we think your heart is starting to form collateral arteries around the block. Sometimes that happens. We want to try medication and exercise and a strict diet, and there is a chance you'll be normal in a year or two, perhaps a bit longer."

"Normal . . ."

"Of course you can't run the Iditarod again."

"Iditarod . . ."

Nothing was working right. I could not think. I simply could not think. I eased my leg and tried to swallow the fear, make the smell of death go away, but it did not and it has not and is with me now while I write this and it will never leave.

"You'll have to live a more normal life."

"Normal . . ."

"You'll take medication, walk briskly every day, and attend a class on diet and nutrition here in the hospital. Of course there are some risks—you do have heart disease. But if you treat it right there is a good chance you'll live for a very long time and everything will be the same . . ."

But he was wrong. Nothing after that time would be the same as it had been before, nothing would be normal.

I had smelled the copper, the flat copper, and I knew that heart disease was the number-one killer— that's how they always put it, the number-one killer, like it was a goddamn contest—the number-one killer of men between fifty and sixty years old. I was coming on fifty and had smelled the copper and it would not ever be the same again nor would I live again.

Not as I lived.

Not with dogs.

And how could that be? How could I live without the sweep of them? Without the blink on the horizon and the snap-joy of them and the reason they gave to life? How in living hell could that be?

All those questions were there then, while he talked wearing the smock with the little Disney figures on it, and they are here now when I am fifty-three, and they will be here tonight as I go to what passes for sleep, and they will be here tomorrow when I awaken.

How can it be to live without the dogs?

Then the hardest thing of all—the phone call to a friend, another dog driver: "You have to come and take them all—pups, dogs, sleds—everything but Cookie. I have to have them gone when I get home or . . ."

Unfinished.

Or I won't do it. Or I'll die. Or I won't be able to stand it.

The break must be clean. He will take good care of them, run the Iditarod with them, run with my dogs.

My dogs. God.

How can it be to live without the dogs?

Other books by Gary Paulsen
published by Harcourt, Inc.
in Harvest paperback editions

CLABBERED DIRT, SWEET GRASS

EASTERN SUN, WINTER MOON

THE MADONNA STORIES